This Little Pig

This
Little
Pig

The Story of Marketing

by

James Playsted Wood

THOMAS NELSON INC.
New York   Camden

Library of Congress Catalog Card Number: 70-164975

International Standard Book Number: 0-8407-6158-9

Printed in the United States of America

for E. C. W.

Acknowledgments

For their generous cooperation in providing data requested, in many instances for their patience in answering detailed questions, may I thank: John F. Brookman, American Dairy Association; Reginald T. Clough, American Education Publications; Bruce Butterfield, American Meat Institute; V. Anne Edlund, American Petroleum Institute; June McSwain, American Forest Institute; Dr. Robert C. Lusk, Automobile Manufacturers Association, Inc.; E. Blair Proctor, The Coca-Cola Company; Robert M. Fuoss, Federated Department Stores, Inc.; John F. Manfredi, General Foods Corporation; General Motors Corporation; Edward V. Callanan, Internal Revenue Service, U.S. Treasury Department; Walter L. Thompson, The International Nickel Company, Inc.; Robert Feinschreiber, National Association of Manufacturers; John Muench, Jr., National Forest Products Association; Dr. Donald M. Hobart, Sea Pines Plantation Company; Catherine McAndrews, Super Market Institute; Gloria R. Mosesson, Thomas Nelson Inc.; Frances Fuller and Dr. Alden C. Manchester, U.S. Department of Agriculture; Fred Isley and Arthur J. Zuckerman, Xerox Corporation.

Contents

1. Early Marketing   *13*
2. The Marketing Function   *24*
3. Department Store Origins   *35*
4. Pricing and Packaging for the Market   *44*
5. Marketing Channels   *53*
6. Marketing of Automobiles   *64*
7. Advertising as Marketing   *78*
8. Mass Marketing: Coca-Cola   *88*
9. Communications Marketing: Xerox   *95*
10. Food Marketing   *104*
11. Chain Store Marketing   *112*
12. Department Store Marketing: Federated   *122*
13. Class Marketing: Sea Pines Plantation   *132*
14. Industrial Marketing: International Nickel   *145*
15. Restrictions on Marketing   *155*
16. Consumer Education   *166*
17. Marketing Research: Conclusion   *173*
    Bibliographical Note   *185*
    Index   *187*

This little pig went to market,

This little pig stayed home,

This little pig had roast beef,

This little pig had none.

And this little pig cried, Wee-wee-wee-wee-wee,

I can't find my way home.

— 1 —

Early Marketing

Robinson Crusoe lived one of the great adventures of all time. With no one to help and no one to hinder, he lived his own life. For over two hundred and fifty years men have admired and sometimes envied his complete independence and self-sufficiency. The English poet William Cowper wrote in words supposed to have been spoken by Alexander Selkirk, who was the real-life Robinson Crusoe,

> I am monarch of all I survey,
>   My right there is none to dispute;
> From the centre all round to the sea
>   I am lord of the fowl and the brute.

For twenty-nine years, ten months, and nineteen days Robinson Crusoe lived alone on an uninhabited island off the northern coast of South America. With courage, resourcefulness, and ingenuity he provided his own food, clothing, and shelter. He bore what often seemed to him his almost unbearable solitude. Until he rescued the cannibal Friday and Friday's father from their captors, who had brought them to his island for a feast, he never saw another human being.

Robinson Crusoe has become the classic example of a man's

fending for himself, pitting his wit and strength against the forces of nature. He built his own "castle" and his "bower" or country estate. He fashioned his own crude clothing for protection against the fierce sun and the tropical rains. He drove off invaders. With his dogs, his cats, his parrot, and his goats, he managed to maintain his health and sanity, even his piety. Everything he did he had to do for himself.

Yet even Robinson Crusoe did not start with nothing. The only man to reach shore alive when his ship was wrecked on a sandbar in a storm in 1650, he had only a knife, a pipe, and a pouch of tobacco when, half drowned, he touched land. In the days following he made trip after trip, eleven in all, back to the ship before it sank. Contriving a rude raft, he brought back clothing, sails, bags of gunpowder, two rusty swords, two fowling pieces (shotguns), some carpenter's tools, cheese, bread, rice, barley, empty casks, his hammock, and cables, hawsers, razors, scissors, and knives. He salvaged Bibles, pen, ink, and paper, charts, books on navigation, and all the ironwork he could pry loose from the 120-ton vessel which had left port with a crew of fourteen besides its captain and his cabin boy.

Crusoe retrieved dozens of hatchets, and needles, pins, thread, spikes, crowbars, and a large stock of brandy which he used for medicinal purposes. He found another shotgun, seven muskets, more powder, and sheets of lead for bullets. He was well armed. "I had the biggest Magazine of all Kinds that ever was laid up, I believe, for one Man."

Least important of all that he recovered from the wreck was thirty pounds in gold and silver coin. He had no place to spend it. There was no market in which he could buy the other tools he needed or replenish the supply of food he soon consumed. It was fortunate for him, and he knew it, that he started out equipped with many of the useful products of civilization which had been bought in various markets. Without them he could have lived but a few days, at most a week or two.

He soon found that all he had saved was pitifully insufficient, and there were no shops from which he could obtain even the simplest necessities. He had to carve his own wooden spade. He had only an ax and an adze to make boards for his castle.

It took him days to cut down a large tree, two more days to chop away the boughs. Then,

> With inexpressible hacking and hewing I reduc'd both Side of it into Chips, till it began to be light enough to move; then I turn'd it, and made one Side of it smooth, and flat, as a Board from End to End; then turning that Side downward, cut the other Side, till I brought the plank to be about three Inches thick. Any one may judge the Labour of my Hands in such a Piece of Work; but Labour and Patience carry'd me through that and many other Things; I only observe this in particular, to show, the Reason why so much of my Time went away with so little work, *viz.* That what might be a little to be done with Help and Tools, was a vast Labour, and requir'd a prodigious Time to do alone, and by Hand.

Robinson Crusoe had to be his own carpenter, hunter, butcher, animal tamer, herdsman, farmer, boatbuilder, sailmaker, potter, chandler (he made his candles from goat tallow), tailor, baker, and mechanic. He could not go to market for rice and barley or pans in which to bake his bread. He could not even do as men have done almost since there were men: trade or swap for what he desperately needed.

For all the time on his island, Robinson Crusoe lived in a world without markets. After he had been there for some years, another ship was wrecked offshore, and in another difficult salvage operation, he got more muskets, gunpowder, a brass kettle, and a gridiron. He was glad of the shirts and handkerchiefs he found and the shoes he took off the feet of drowned men, but a treasure trove of doubloons and pieces of eight was meaningless. " . . . for as to the money, I had no manner of Occasion for it; 'Twas to me as the Dirt under my Feet; and I would have given it all for three or four pair of *English* Shoes and Stockings, which were Things I greatly wanted, but had not had on my Feet now for many years."

Men living under pioneer conditions have experienced some of the difficulties Robinson Crusoe knew. When the first English settlers landed in America, they had with them only the clothes they wore and the few possessions they were able to bring. The *Mayflower* touched at the tip of Cape Cod before it sailed on down to Plymouth. At what became Provincetown the seaworn Pilgrims looked about them and saw only sea and wilderness. As Governor Bradford wrote in his diary, " . . . they now had no friends to welcome them nor inns to entertain and refresh their weatherbeaten bodies; no houses or much less towns to repair to to seek for succour." He might have added that there were no markets in which to purchase food or buy materials to build their homes. Years later William Bradford's son wrote that there was everything to do, as in the beginning of the world.

The first settlers had to catch fish and shoot deer and turkey for food. They learned from the Indians how to grow corn. They built their own log houses, cut boards in sawpits, thatched their roofs, grew herbs and vegetables as they developed their gardens. Every man had to be a farmer and his own blacksmith, veterinarian, carpenter, and cabinetmaker as well. Families ate and drank what they raised or killed themselves. They spun and wove flax and wool for their clothing. At first there were no markets, for men had nothing to sell or to trade.

This was an unnatural situation for them. Europeans had always known markets where they could buy or barter for what they wished. Trade is as old as recorded history. The Babylonians, the Phoenicians, the Egyptians, the Greeks, and the Romans were all traders. Both Rome and Athens had their shops and markets.

Ancient Rome was crowded with small shops, run usually by the owner and his wife with the help of a slave or two. As shopkeepers on the side streets of American cities do today, the proprietor stood in the doorway crying his wares and trying to buttonhole customers. Again like the small shopkeeper today, Roman merchants shuttered their shops at night against thieves. Some people at the time thought the shopkeepers were the thieves. Cicero is quoted as saying, "All retail dealers may be described as dishonest and base, for the dealer will gain nothing except by profuse lying, and nothing is more disgraceful than untruthful huckstering."

The great merchant traders of the medieval world sailed their fleets to the ends of the known earth for gold and spices, or anything they could find and bring to market. Venice was a center of trade centuries before it became a tourist attraction. The new world was discovered by traders seeking new routes to the riches of the East and settled by European powers competing for gold, fish, fur, and other spoils. Trade has always been the concomitant and sometimes the precursor of civilization. Wars have been fought for trade advantage. The American West was opened by men hunting gold and furs. Russia discovered Alaska in its search for ivory and pelts which it sold in the rich markets of China.

Marketing as selling saved the first British colonies established on the Atlantic coast. The Virginia Company established Jamestown under Captain John Smith in 1607 in the expectation of obtaining gold. When after a year none was forthcoming and the company had received no return on its investment, it issued an ultimatum. Jamestown must ship back to the company's office in England products to the value of the eight thousand dollars the Virginia Company had expended in founding it, or company support of the colony would cease.

There was no gold in Virginia, but there were pines. Captain John Smith set thirty men to cutting down trees and sawing them into planks and boards. He had other men burn pine wood to make the potash used in the manufacture of glass and soap. Jamestown sent a cargo of lumber, timber for ships' masts, potash, tar, and turpentine back to England, and the

Virginia Company was mollified. The marketing of wood and wood products can be said to be the first American industry. It is still one of the most important industries in the United States.

The New England colonies as well as Virginia marketed lumber to their English backers, but their principal support was another natural product, fish, for which there was a strong and continuous market in the Catholic countries of Europe. The Sacred Cod is sacred in Massachusetts because of its leading role in support of the economy of Plymouth and Massachusetts Bay.

The impulse to trade seems to be imbedded in human nature. Primitive man traded object for object. In earlier stages of his development, man traded a horse for a cow, one wife for another, or gold, trinkets, and domesticated animals for several wives. When the United States was still primarily an agricultural country, men traded muscle and goodwill, neighbors gathering to help a fellow farmer with his haying or threshing. In his turn he helped them with their reaping or barn raising. The penchant of boys for trading is known to everyone who ever was a boy or ever saw one. A battered baseball for a slingshot—why not? Once it may have been a torn toga for a clay pot. It can come to be the swapping of the chassis of an abandoned jalopy for a coil for a Model A. Modern man still likes to trade, to swap a rifle for a camera, no-longer-used golf clubs for an outboard motor in need of repair.

The principle is simple. You exchange something you no longer need for what you feel you must have. You are "in the market" for a fox terrier or a football, and your market is where it is and who has it. Newspapers and folksy magazines still carry swap columns: a tuxedo for a bookcase or what have you; ten rose bushes for some three-year old spruce; companionship for room and board. Drugstore and university-dormitory bulletin boards carry neatly typed or hastily scribbled notices of what someone will swap for what.

The simple trade of object for object or service for service persists, but long ago people discovered that it is generally more convenient to trade for the wherewithal to obtain some other item desired; that is, to buy and sell for currency of some kind that has an established value—money.

People discovered, too, the convenience—and profit—of assembling goods in one market where they could sell and buyers could spend just what they wished. Great annual fairs were held in many places in medieval Europe. There were splendid fairs in France at Lyons, at Aix-la-Chapelle, at Champagne, and at Brie. The Count of Flanders established fairs at Bruges and Courtrai. Merchants brought their goods from many countries to these fairs, which often went on for weeks. Acrobats, jugglers, dancers, and pickpockets plied their arts at the fairs. There were clowns and tumblers and stalls bursting with delights. You could buy corn, silk, spices, and slaves. One year at an eleventh-century German fair seven thousand Danish captives were placed on sale.

The greatest fair in England was established in Stourbridge in A.D. 207 and ran for centuries. The same Daniel Defoe who wrote *Robinson Crusoe* described the Stourbridge Fair as he saw it in 1723. Large wholesalers of grain and other staples had their wares for sale, and business was done on an international scale. That part of the Stourbridge Fair was like a convention of buyers and sellers today.

Then, the main street of the Stourbridge Fair was Cheapside. For a half mile, the length of the cornfield in which the fair was held, Cheapside was lined with the booths and stalls of braziers, turners, milliners, haberdashers, toymakers, confectioners, pastry cooks, and vendors of all kinds. Clowns performed, and fortunetellers looked into the future. Horse traders tried to outwit each other. Stourbridge was a super-supermarket of eighteenth-century England.

Today in the United States, people crowd the regional, state, and county fairs to see the biggest pumpkins, the prize apple pies, the newest farm machinery, and the horse and automobile races, and to spill out their happiness and their money in games of chance. Usually every year there is a multi-million-dollar world's fair somewhere, with nations competing in the marketplace.

We all know of markets from our earliest years. As babies we crow with delight as someone counts our toes.

> This little pig went to market,
> This little pig stayed home . . .

We laugh and shout for joy as someone seated with crossed legs holds our hands and bounces us up and down on his foot to the song:

> To market, to market, to buy a fat pig,
> Home again, home again, jiggety-jig;
> To market, to market, to buy a fat hog,
> Home again, home again, jiggety-jog!

Early, we associate marketing with pleasure. The market is crowded, noisy, and gay. Better than that, it is the place where you can get cake, candy, cookies, toys, and all the shiny and sweet-smelling things any child could desire.

Even for adults, markets are pleasure. Men meet and talk on the floor of the great stock exchanges and in the commodity exchanges. There is the excitement of possible gain, the fear of possible loss. Women forgather at the vegetable market, the fish market, the flower market, or, more likely, the all-encompassing supermarket, to see their friends and to gossip as well as to shop. The market is not just an economic necessity. It is a place for relaxation as well as for buying—which often is a relaxation in itself. Spending is a kind of pleasure.

An old Italian proverb says, "Three women and a goose make a market." It is fun for all, except, eventually, for the goose. In 1640 the English religious poet George Herbert wrote ruefully, "The market is the best garden." He found better fruits, vegetables, and flowers there than he could raise. In 1616 Nicholas Breton included a shrewd comment in his *Outlandish Proverbs:* "Good wares make good markets." This is still true.

Marketing, then, is very old in human experience and a natural activity which we know from early childhood. What we know about, of course, is just one side of marketing, and marketing is always a two-way process. It is selling as well as buying. From the viewpoint of those engaged in it as a profession or a means of livelihood, marketing is mostly selling. The English have an accurate phrase. They say that a man is "in trade" when they mean that he is in business. That is all any business is—trade. The farmer trades his produce, the lawyer his knowledge, the doctor his skill, every employed man and woman his time and labor for money. Each trades what he has for what he wants, whether it is a country estate or a slice of chewing gum.

Robinson Crusoe himself was in trade. He was a marketer. After leaving his home in York against the wishes of his parents, he took forty pounds' worth of toys and trifles to the Guinea coast and traded them for gold, for which he received three hundred English pounds in London. Following other adventures, he became a sugar planter in Brazil. When he was shipwrecked, he was on his way to Africa for himself and as agent for other planters to trade his cargo of hatchets and other tools and toys for slaves. This was legitimate trade in the seventeenth century. Regardless of color, slavery had been an accepted and understood part of life for centuries. The Greeks and then the Romans enslaved their captives. Wars were fought just to take prisoners, who were then enslaved. The Moslems had an established and thriving slave trade in Christians. Captured by Turks, Robinson Crusoe himself had been a slave for two years before he escaped and was rescued by a kindly Portuguese sea captain who took him to Brazil.

In Brazil, Crusoe imported British goods and sold them at high profit. He grew sugarcane and tobacco which he sold profitably in markets abroad. Four years of such marketing had made him wealthy. He had left Brazil with his head full of schemes to grow even wealthier through trade. For nearly thirty years he lived in a marketless world only because he had no choice. He returned to the world of marketing as soon as he could after his release from his island.

Women used to go marketing with their shopping baskets and return with them filled with meat, eggs, vegetables, and whatever their families needed. They go to the shopping center now in their station wagons or family sedans in just the same way. From their viewpoint, that is marketing. From the viewpoint of the seller, marketing is taking products to the place where they can be sold.

When I was a small boy spending the summer in the country with my family, I often went to market with the farmer at whose home we boarded. He'd harness his team (the horses were called Harry and Dolly), and we'd drive from his Dutchess County farm into Poughkeepsie with a big wagonload of tomatoes. There his market was the housewives in the residential streets. We always took sandwiches along, but the most important part of our lunch was the small blueberry or custard pies we bought from a baker's cart. Pies never tasted better—and we were part of the baker's market on those days. In mid- or late afternoon, baskets emptied of tomatoes, Harry and Dolly ambled home with their lighter load.

That is marketing at its simplest. The farmer who raised them sold his tomatoes directly to the families who ate them. Marketing is usually a far more complicated process. It is not just one man selling from house to house and close to home, but millions of men and women distributing the millions of products made by other millions of men and women. Economic activity of this kind is usually divided into production and distribution, that is, into the making and then the making available of what has been produced. The two are complementary, one as important as the other.

If the nail remains where it is made, say, on a side street in Pittsburgh or a small town in Connecticut, it is of little use to the carpenter in Anchorage, Alaska. If the gallon of crude oil stays where it is pumped up from some well in Texas or Saudi

Arabia, the family car in New York or California does not go very well. If shoes never leave the warehouse next to the factory in Brockton, Massachusetts, or Flowery Branch, Georgia, you might have to go barefoot. Your television set might not work very well without components made in Japan. If advertising had not told you they exist, you might never have heard of electric refrigerators or oil heat or ballpoint pens.

Marketing in all its many phases is of such basic value and significance in the United States that more people are engaged in it than in the whole of production. It is inescapable. It affects all of us every day and throughout our lives.

— 2 —

The Marketing Function

Marketing is selling. It is selling as seen, understood, and practiced by the seller.

There are those engaged in it who will disagree strongly with this definition. They consider marketing to be much more comprehensive. They feel that it includes all of the many activities that go into the origin as well as the distribution of a product, with selling only a part of the marketing whole. The American Marketing Association says that marketing is "those business activities involved in the flow of goods from production to consumption."

Widen your definition of selling to take in not just the actual transaction between a seller and a buyer but also all the planning and activities at every stage of the process of getting something salable made and sold, and selling and marketing do mean the same thing. The final sale is the end of all trade. Unless you can sell the tire chains, pins and needles, or guided missiles, you can't stay in business very long. You cannot just manufacture paper or paint and let it pile up. What you make has to go to people who will buy and use it, then buy more, in order for you to keep your factory going, pay your employees, pay your taxes, pay your expenses, and still have enough left to feed, shelter, and clothe your family and yourself.

In practice, "marketing," "selling," and "distribution" are used interchangeably. There are no sharp divisions among them. They merge indistinguishably into one another.

Marketing can and often does begin even before there is a product to market, sell, or distribute. It may start when a man or woman has an idea for something that he can obtain, make, or have made—some object that people will buy.

It may start just the other way. Someone may decide that a market exists for something—say, a new cereal which he can describe as having a violet-scented squeak and squish distinct from the ordinary snap, crackle, and pop. He must then locate the ingredients, build or rent factories for quantity production, and find wholesalers to handle the new cereal and retailers to sell it to consumers who will eat it. Even before a package of it exists, the inspired marketer may plan the advertising and promotion which will convince great numbers of people that violet-scented Squeak and Squish will make them healthy, wealthy, wise, and free to do as they please anywhere, at any time.

There is the idea, widely disseminated in marketing circles, that a product should be made, priced, packaged, and distributed with the buyer in mind from the first. Because the sale *is* the ultimate goal, this makes good sense. This is called dynamic marketing.

The opposite way—call it static or undynamic marketing, if you like—is to make a good product, then wait for people to come and buy it. You can make an ax so well designed that it fits your hand perfectly. It has perfect balance, a head of the best steel, and a handle of heart oak. You can temper the blade so that it never loses its edge, and wedge head and handle so that they can never separate. You can do all this yet fail if people decide they no longer want axes, prefer a cheaper ax, or never hear of your ax. Many men and businesses have failed because they made automobiles, pencils, or tinware that were excellent in quality but did not satisfy the needs or whims of possible buyers.

The peddlers—some of them itinerant monks—who trudged the highways and byways of England in the Middle Ages did not carry wares that people would not buy. They sold pardons, charms, amulets, tin, and pottery, any objects that they knew in advance the peasantry would purchase. These peddlers practiced a kind of canny marketing. Their nineteenth-century successors did not carry coals to Newcastle, for Newcastle had almost all the coal there was.

In the United States, the earliest marketers were Europeans who traded with, and usually cheated, the Indians. They had lucrative markets for all the beaver, fox, mink, and other pelts they could obtain. In return they gave the Indians trinkets at first, then what they knew the Indians most wanted, guns and liquor. They were shrewd marketers too.

The traders were followed by the peddlers. They stocked up in the cities of the East with whatever they thought they could sell in the settlements of the westward-moving frontier, and they could sell almost anything, for demand far outran supply. These Yankee peddlers went everywhere. Amos Bronson Alcott, father of the author of *Little Women,* was one of them. From Spindle Hill in Wolcott, Connecticut, Alcott traveled not west but south into Virginia and the Carolinas. He walked hundreds of miles from plantation to plantation carrying two heavy tin trunks. They were laden with thimbles, thread, scissors, knives, cloth, pencils, spectacles, razor strops, and even a few books.

Bronson Alcott spent about five years peddling, and he was not alone. So many peddlers came from Connecticut that it became known as the Nutmeg State; it was believed that Connecticut Yankees could sell anything, and the legend arose that they sold wooden nutmegs. The fragrant nutmeg, which is grated for use, is the pit of the fruit of a tropical tree, but, so it was said, ingenious Connecticut artisans fashioned them out of wood and peddled them to the unsuspecting as the genuine article.

Other peddlers set out from the hill villages of western

Massachusetts, where mint, which grows there in profusion, was distilled into essences in a thriving home industry. They added a selection of knickknacks to their store of small bottles of spearmint, peppermint, and cologne and took to the roads. Nathaniel Hawthorne met one of these peddlers from Ashfield on a stagecoach in 1838. The man had sold out all his stock in about three weeks and was returning home for more. He told Hawthorne enthusiastically that peddling sure beat farming.

These enterprising Yankee peddlers gained such a reputation that even Mark Twain knew of them and wrote:

> When I was a boy in the back settlements of the Mississippi Valley, where a gracious and beautiful Sunday-school simplicity and unpracticality prevailed, the "Yankee" (citizen of the New England States) was hated with a splendid energy. . . . In a trade, the Yankee was held to be about five times the match of the Westerner. His shrewdness, his insight, his judgment, his knowledge, his enterprise, and his formidable cleverness in applying these forces were frankly confessed and most competently cursed.

In the cities and towns of the East, markets and shops sprang up after the pattern which the colonists had known in England. Boston had many shops in the eighteenth century. One of the shopkeepers was the silversmith Paul Revere, who made, advertised, and sold false teeth as well as silverware. At first most of the goods in the shops came from Europe, for the colonies manufactured little. Then goods of local artisans were for sale locally. Travel and transportation were too difficult to make seeking larger markets feasible. The peddlers who ventured away from the centers of population a little later went by ship, then by foot or by horse and wagon, and their only stock was what they could carry.

People did things for themselves. The local blacksmith made the spades, axes, and hoes for the local farmers. The miller ground their grain. The tanner turned hides into leather for his village customers.

Two forces changed all this. The Industrial Revolution turned what had been home industries—spinning, weaving, dyeing, even distilling—into factory production in the beginning of mass manufacturing. The developing railroads made it possible to ship large quantities of grain, liquor, hardware, clothing, paper, and other products greater distances. Hordes of immigrants poured in from Europe and settled in the cities of the East or pressed westward to the opening farmlands. In the fast-growing United States of the nineteenth century, with people farming, lumbering, mining, and ever pressing westward, there was a market for everything from plows and pistols to pianos and powder puffs.

Some of the peddlers settled down in towns that had been on their routes. They opened shops, stocked them with staples and fancy goods, and became independent merchants—who fought off the depredations of peddlers such as they had been as the evil deeds of foreign interlopers. Soon a fabled race of men succeeded most of the peddlers. These were the now almost legendary traveling salesmen and drummers, the representatives of manufacturers and distributors in many lines who called on the retail trade and took the shopkeepers' orders.

They called on the larger city stores and on the general stores and specialty shops that were springing up in towns everywhere. They did not have to sell very hard. Often they just had to take orders two or three times a year. The shops needed everything: crackers, lard, bacon, guns, canned goods, bonnets, even such luxuries as jewelry for those who struck it rich in mining, lumbering, railroading, or ranching. Less and less was homemade now; more and more was "store-bought."

There was little brand-name merchandise. Men wanted tools and guns, and women household necessities. They did not care who made them as long as the articles were satisfactory. Most manufacturers did not bother to put their names on what they made either as advertisement or guarantee. One of the first articles to be known and asked for by name has often been credited with helping to open the West.

Born in Hartford, Connecticut, in 1814, Samuel Colt worked as a boy in his father's textile factory. He left when he was sixteen to ship as a sailor on a long voyage to India. On this voyage he whittled out of wood his idea for a pistol with a revolving chamber. After a year at sea he returned to work in a bleachery owned by his father, but soon left to work on his gun. In 1831 he made two revolvers and applied for a patent the next year. He got it finally in 1836 and formed a company to manufacture the Colt revolver in Paterson, New Jersey. He tried to interest the government in his new weapon, but the government was indifferent. The business failed in 1842.

It was not until a trapped officer shot his way out of ambush in the Mexican War which began in 1846 that the United States Army ordered one thousand Colt revolvers. Samuel Colt seized on this to advertise and promote his six-shooter. He took out patents on improvements and went into quantity manufacture in Whitneyville, Connecticut, then in Hartford. This time his business grew rapidly as men learned the advantages of the Colt, and he built a huge armory in Hartford to meet the demand.

Manufacturers were beginning to advertise intently and extensively by the mid-nineteenth century. They affixed their names or trademarks to what they made, branded their articles, then told the world of the virtues of their products. They advertised to create markets at the same time that they created the articles themselves. In a phrase often used, they manufactured customers as they manufactured products.

There was a surge of business after the Civil War, as there is after most wars. The war had acted to increase industrial capacity in the North and to increase transportation facilities. A pent-up demand for all kinds of merchandise had been created by four years of scarcity while men were fighting and factories given over to the manufacture of military matériel. Manufacturers competed for sales and profit.

In the late 1860's the sedate *Atlantic Monthly* carried advertisements for all kinds of patent medicines, most of them promising miraculous cures. It had advertisements for Steinway pianos—grand, square, and upright. In large space in large type, complete with a picture of its inventor, the Howe sewing machine was billed as "The Oldest Machine in the World." The pages of the *Atlantic* touted Clark's thread, Tiffany jewelry, and Turner's Tic Doulereux, "The Undoubted Cure for All Excrutiating Ills Known as Neuralgia or Nervous Ache." Nursing bottles, wagons, carriages, carpeting, life insurance, books of all kinds, shoe polish, carpet sweepers, and hair dressings competed in the pages of the *Atlantic* and of other magazines and in the newspapers.

Ralph Waldo Emerson is reputed to have said, "If a man can write a better book, preach a better sermon, or make a better mouse-trap than his neighbor, though he builds his house in the woods, the world will make a beaten path to his door."

This is true, provided the world learns of the mousetrap, that experience with it proves that it really will catch mice, and the inventor is not out-advertised by competitors who make an inferior mousetrap. Samuel Colt had made a better pistol, but the world did not beat a path to his door until satisfactory use and widespread publicity told people about it. If the mice-harried world does not know about the mousetrap in the woods, it will not seek it out or buy it.

Emerson wrote of the attitude that prevailed in the world of commerce during the early years of his life. The post–Civil War period changed that attitude. Manufacturers, wholesalers, and retailers—particularly manufacturers—sought markets to absorb the goods they made and distributed.

The change was really only in degree. Makers and sellers have always sought buyers, but now they sought them on a national scale and in sharp competition for large sales and large profits. Dynamic marketing really got its start now—the deliberate appeal to the customer and the construction of markets simultaneously with the production of branded goods.

That is the modern marketing approach, and it would have

changed everything for Emerson's mousetrap maker. If his trap
was well made and deadly, brightly colored and well advertised,
its maker would have to build factories in his woods and go
into assembly-line production to meet the demand. Then the
purchasers would rush in, and, today, so would the government
investigators, tax men, tourists, and protesters. They would
not only beat a path to his door, but probably despoil the woods,
and perhaps destroy his house and burn his stock-in-trade. If
he survived the attention of today's society, the mousetrap
maker would probably spend his old age repenting his inven-
tiveness and attempt to benefit mankind—but he would have
reached his market.

Sometimes markets can be materialized out of little but
emotion. People are terrified into buying deodorants and breath
sweeteners for fear they offend. They are persuaded to eat
tasteless food because they are told it is good for them and to
swallow placebos—harmless but ineffective medicinal concoc-
tions—because they have been insistently informed that they will
restore youth or grant an approximation of immortality.

Sometimes markets can almost literally be created out of
nothing. People made fun of Timothy Dexter of Newbury-
port, Massachusetts, when in the eighteenth century he sent
eight shiploads of brass bed-warming pans with long wooden
handles to the hot West Indies. Timothy Dexter laughed last.
The West Indians bought them to use in skimming boiling
sugarcane syrup and to fry fish and yams over open fires, and
the enterprising Mr. Dexter made a large profit.

In one of his short stories in *Cabbages and Kings,* O. Henry
shows how a profitable market can be concocted out of nothing
more than expertly applied imagination and skulduggery.

Billy Keogh and John de Graffenreid Atwood are in tropical
Coralia, where Atwood is United States consul, and they are
bored. They are particularly bored with answering foolish
inquiries from foolish Americans. When a letter arrives from
Atwood's uncle, postmaster in Galesburg, Alabama, saying that

one of its citizens has inquired about the profit possibilities of opening a shoe store in Coralia, the two men answer with malicious humor aforethought. They give a glowing account of the possibilities, saying that with its considerable population Coralia does not have a single shoe store. They forgot to mention that none of the natives wore, had ever worn, or had any wish to wear shoes.

To their amazement and consternation, the inquirer took their answer seriously. He sold all his worldly goods, invested his life savings of four thousand dollars in shoes, and landed in Coralia with enough cases of stock, Keogh reported, to shoe the entire population of South America down to Tierra del Fuego. He also brought his daughter, with whom Atwood was in love. Aghast at the success of their humor, the perpetrators were faced with finding a way out. It took Atwood all night to solve the problem, but in the morning he cabled Galesburg one hundred dollars for a rush order of five hundred pounds of cockleburs.

Modern marketing could hardly stoop to such underfoot methods. With giant corporations achieving annual sales in the billions of dollars and comparatively pigmy-sized companies making net sales in the millions every year—with mammoth conglomerates and heterogeneous combines in place of the peddlers and small merchants of the last century—such crude, if effective, measures would be a little undignified.

Marketing today has at its command established and constantly improved methods of mass production and dissemination. It has experts in the design of products and of the containers in which they are packed. It has computers to carry out intricate cost accounting and to tabulate the results of marketing research. It has highly sophisticated electronic means of mass communications, as well as mere paper and print and billboards, for sales promotion and advertising.

Marketing has something even better in the United States. It has a population nearing 225 million, an affluent people with the means to buy not only necessities but also luxuries. Marketing has staples, new products, improved products, and the seemingly infinite capacity of industry to produce and consumers to absorb what they need, what they do not need, what they can be taught to need, and what they will never need but insist upon having.

In marketing terminology there are no people. People eat, sleep, and variously disport themselves. They do many other things, but marketing is interested in them only as they buy and use, and use up and buy again whatever is for sale. In marketing terminology, people are consumers.

Marketing counts consumers, locates them, scrutinizes them, evaluates their potentials and their performance as buyers, and tries to reach them with every means it can use and every enticement it can devise. Marketing exploits consumers, but it also serves them. Marketing gets products from where they are planned and made to people who wish them in quantity and at prices they can and will pay.

Marketing does this for individual consumers. It does more for consumers collectively by underwriting and supporting the national economy.

Without mass consumption there can be no mass production, and the United States is geared to mass production. In order to keep industry operative and all the people in it employed, marketing must sell what industry makes. Marketing supports everyone engaged in distribution in all its stages—transportation, wholesaling, retailing, advertising, accounting, research, and all the other parts of the whole. The support of marketing enables both production and distribution workers to be consumers.

The successful marketing of what is produced also supports the more than 11.2 million federal, state, and local government civilian employees—a number about equivalent to the total population of Maine, New Hampshire, Vermont, Massachusetts, Rhode Island, and Connecticut. These employees neither produce nor distribute, but, together with uncounted additional numbers supported by government grants and projects or employed through government contracts, they are all consumers. They depend wholly, if indirectly through taxation, on the economic system established and maintained by trade and based upon marketing to fulfill their needs.

— 3 —
Department Store Origins

Small children in the City of New York used to have an invaluable rhyme. You could use it in skipping rope, in choosing sides for games, in counting out to see who was "it," and, followed by "Ready or not, here I come," in hide-and-seek. It went like this:

Ten-amaker
Nine-amaker
Eight-amaker
Seven-amaker
Six-amaker
Five-amaker
Four-amaker
Three-amaker
Two-amaker
WANAMAKER!

Almost every child in New York and Philadelphia knew the Wanamaker name and what it stood for. They knew it because their parents knew it, because they heard it continually, and because—unless they were very unfortunate—they had been to Wanamaker's at least once and perhaps many times.

They also knew it because John Wanamaker made sure, or as nearly as he could, that everyone in the country knew it.

Son of a bricklayer, John Wanamaker was born in Philadelphia in 1838. When he was fourteen years old, he became an errand boy in a bookstore. He gave that up to work in a men's clothing store; and at nineteen gave that up to become the first paid secretary of the Y.M.C.A. In 1861, when he was twenty-two years old, John Wanamaker opened a men's store in partnership with his brother-in-law, Nathan Brown.

From the very first, John Wanamaker was a marketing man *par excellence*. He went after customers even before the new store was ready to open. They named the store Wanamaker & Brown's Oak Hall, and Wanamaker scattered throughout Philadelphia teaser handbills which said only "W. & B." When people's curiosity had been aroused, he followed that with a second handbill announcing the opening of Oak Hall. Until 1953, when blocks of buildings were torn down to enlarge the parks about Independence Hall, the name Oak Hall could still be seen sunk in bronze letters into the pavement on the southwest corner of Sixth and Market streets.

Oak Hall took in $20.67 the first day. Wanamaker kept the sixty-seven cents but spent the rest to advertise in the *Philadelphia Public Ledger* a sale of men's suits at $3.00 each.

Wanamaker bought cheaply and sold cheaply. The Civil War was on, so he sold uniforms as well as civilian clothes, and he advertised flamboyantly. Besides newspaper and poster advertising, he went in for spectaculars of many kinds. He loosed great balloons and gave free suits to anyone who captured one. He organized parades of men wearing wire frames shaped like yachts with "Oak Hall" flying on their pennants. He built "Wanamaker" signs a hundred feet long alongside the railroad tracks coming into Philadelphia. He dressed employees in hunting costumes and sent them out on the highways, often for a week at a time, blowing horns from coaches drawn by six horses. Within ten years, Oak Hall was the largest retail men's clothing store in the United States.

Nathan Brown died in 1868. The next year, John Wanamaker opened another store on more fashionable Chestnut Street. In 1876, with all the fanfare and publicity he could devise or obtain, he opened a huge department store in what had been a railroad freight depot at Thirteenth and Market streets. Wanamaker's in Philadelphia is still at that location, the store running through a long city block to Chestnut.

Wanamaker stocked his "Grand Depot" with a half million dollars' worth of men's clothing and dry goods—"dry-goods stores" were so called to distinguish them from the many which sold liquor. After long and loud advance publicity he opened to a crowd of nearly seventy thousand. The Centennial Exposition was drawing great crowds to Philadelphia. Curious visitors from all over the world went to see the Grand Depot, and many remained to buy. After the Exposition closed, Wanamaker tried to get other merchants to rent space in the vast converted freight terminal. When this failed, he bought new merchandise of many kinds, opened new departments that were really specialty shops, and Wanamaker's became one of the great department stores.

The idea was not new; it was more than three hundred years old. London had its first department store in 1569. It was Gresham's Royal Burse or Exchange in Cornhill, a collection of specialty shops selling clothes, shoes, foods, jewels, and other items. In 1614 its hardware department, a space only seven and a half by five feet, was rented by an ironmonger (hardware dealer) named Izaak Walton. Walton was the gentle fisherman whose *Compleat Angler,* published in 1653, made him one of the best known of all English writers.

There were earlier department stores in the United States, too. The first is supposed to have been opened in Duxbury, Massachusetts, by James T. Ford & Co. in 1826. (The "Co." was James's brothers, Nathaniel and Peleg.) In a seaport town, the store stocked and sold a miscellany of merchandise: whale oil, wigs, gunpowder and shot, nails, tents, meat, candy, hay cutters, and sundries.

The largest department store in the country when Wanamaker opened his in Philadelphia was A. T. Stewart's in New York. Born in County Antrim, Ireland, Alexander Turney Stewart opened a one-room store on lower Broadway in 1823. Business was good. He moved to a larger store, then to one still larger. A canny businessman, Stewart bought bankrupt stocks at auction, sold his goods reasonably, and thrived. In 1848 he built a new building on Broadway at Chambers Street, just north of City Hall, and went into wholesale and retail dry goods, catering to the wealthy and fashionable.

A. T. Stewart established important merchandising policies. He charged one price to all in a day when bargaining and haggling often set the price. He exchanged goods when customers were dissatisfied. He made cash refunds. He insisted that all customers be treated courteously by his salespeople. Stewart's honesty, tact, and marketing acumen paid him handsomely. In 1862, at what was then the tremendous cost of nearly $2,750,000, he built an eight-story building of brick and stone which covered the entire city block between Broadway and Fourth Avenue and Ninth and Tenth streets. This was far uptown then.

Stewart employed about two thousand people in this store. Business expenses ran to about a million dollars a year, but his sales—wholesale and retail at Chamber Street and retail at Ninth—ran into the many millions. During the Civil War, he had large Army and Navy contracts. With an income averaging $2 million a year, he bought mills in New England, New York, and New Jersey for the manufacture of his own cotton, silk, and woolen goods—blankets, carpets, ribbons, and thread. To supply the largest store in the world he established offices and warehouses in Ireland, Scotland, France, Germany, and Switzerland.

A. T. Stewart became one of the first great "merchant princes." These most fortunate of men lived in sumptuous mansions, had their coaches and yachts, indulged in civic enterprises and philanthropies. Though he paid the lowest wages possible, Stewart donated generously to charities. During the famine of 1847, he sent a shipload of provisions to Ireland, brought the ship back packed with immigrants, and found jobs for most of them. During the Civil War he gave a check for $100,000 to the Sanitary Commission. He sent a shipload of flour to stricken France after its defeat by Prussia in 1871.

John Wanamaker imitated Stewart's one-price policy, his exchanges and refunds, his courtesy to customers, and his buying and marketing practices, but he differed from him in one important respect. Stewart let his stores, the quality of his goods, and his actions speak for themselves. His newspaper advertisements were simple announcements. Wanamaker, who soon had his own millions and his own marble palace, never ceased strenuous advertising. Until the 1920's, his signed editorial advocating the Sunday School virtues appeared daily in Wanamaker advertisements which covered the entire back pages of the New York and Philadelphia newspapers.

A. T. Stewart died the year John Wanamaker opened his Grand Depot. In 1896, Wanamaker bought what had been Stewart's in New York. In both Philadelphia and New York, Wanamaker's became not only great department stores marketing thousands of products—cheap merchandise, quality goods, expensive items, commonplace articles, and rare offerings—but well-known institutions. In both ornately decorated stores, there were concerts and organ recitals. "Meet me at the fountain" was the Wanamaker slogan in New York, where a fountain played in the center of the street floor. In Philadelphia it was "Meet me at the eagle." A large golden eagle stands in a circular space in the ground floor center, the light falling on it from the galleries of the floors above.

A bronze plaque at the Broadway entrance in New York reads proudly, "formerly A. T. Stewart." Wanamaker's, which came to be two large buildings bridged high over the street, remained in this same location long after the New York shopping center had moved north to Thirty-fourth Street and spread on to Forty-second. It was closed in 1955 and, as large city buildings are apt to do when they do not become parking lots, became more government offices. Wanamaker's retailing in the New York area was dispersed into the suburbs and a smaller store in the downtown Manhattan financial district.

The nineteenth century and the early twentieth saw the rise of the city department stores. The Franklin County village of Conway in the foothills of the Berkshires has a small neoclassical library, the Field Memorial Library. Marshall Field was born in Conway in 1834. When he was seventeen, Field went to work in the dry-goods store of Deacon Davis in the larger town of Pittsfield. Five years later he left for Chicago, where he took a job at $400 a year in the wholesale dry-goods firm of Cooley, Wadsworth & Company. By sleeping in the store and spending as little as he could, he saved half his salary. He moved up to become a traveling salesman, then a partner. Potter Palmer had started a fashionable women's store in Chicago in 1852. When he retired, he sold an interest to Marshall Field in what then became Field, Palmer, & Leiter, "Successors to P. Palmer."

Field adopted the Stewart-Wanamaker policies and principles. He added others. He bought and sold only quality merchandise, and he sold goods on approval. Anything could be returned for full value. In 1868 Field and Leiter rented a large building on State Street from Potter and staged a grand opening of the new store. They made their marketing appeal to the wealthy, sent buyers abroad for the latest women's fashions, and imported them direct to Chicago. Chicago women had the newest Paris fashions as quickly as the women in New York and Boston.

Field was a shrewd marketer. He bought for cash, then advertised to create a demand for what he had purchased, then sold for cash or for credit, insisting on prompt payment when bills were due. In this way he was able to undersell competitors. As the business grew, Field contracted for the entire output of certain manufacturers. Later he began to manufacture some of the goods he sold on State Street. A hard worker, Field chose capable managers, exercised tight discipline over his staff, and began store deliveries by boy messengers, then by handcart, then by wagon. Soon Field, Leiter & Company were doing a business of $12 million a year.

The store was burned out in the Chicago fire of 1871, but Field managed to save most of its stock. It became the nucleus of a new store, with another grand opening. Another fire in 1877, another grand opening. In 1881, when he was forty-seven years old and a very wealthy man, Field bought out his partner for $2.5 million. The store, which by this time had doubled its sales annually to $24 million, thus became Marshall Field & Company and one of the world's great mercantile establishments.

Marshall Field caught cold while playing golf in the snow with red balls (as Rudyard Kipling liked to do when he lived in Vermont). Field's golfing partner that day in 1906 was Robert Todd Lincoln, president of the powerful Pullman Company. Despite his illness, Field insisted on taking a business trip to New York. He died there of pneumonia, leaving an estate valued at $120 million. This, of course, was in real money and not subject to income or inheritance taxes.

Gimbel Brothers started in Vincennes, Indiana, in 1842, and opened in Milwaukee in 1887, in Philadelphia in 1894, and in New York in 1909. It purchased the Saks Company in 1923 and opened Saks Fifth Avenue. Jordan Marsh was founded in Boston in 1851. The notorious Jim Fisk, who helped Daniel Drew wreck the Erie Railroad, then joined with Drew and Jay Gould in a conspiracy to corner the gold market, had been first a salesman, then a partner in Jordan Marsh. Rich's, the largest and most important department store in the South, got started in 1867, when a Young Hungarian Jewish peddler named Morris Rich settled in war-devastated Atlanta. He began to sell corsets for fifty cents and stockings for twenty-five in a small shop hastily built of pine boards. Women could not always pay in cash for their stockings and corsets then, so Morris Rich took chickens, eggs, and corn in barter.

"The Biggest Store in the World" started almost as simply. Raymond Hussey Macy was an adventurous young man. Of a Massachusetts mercantile family, he shipped aboard a whaler. Then he prospected for gold in California. In 1858 he opened a small dry-goods store on Sixth Avenue near Fourteenth Street. On just two long counters he sold handkerchiefs, ribbons, embroidery, gloves, stockings, and a few sundries. He expanded into men's furnishings. Then he added pots, pans, jewelry, clocks, silverware, books. He began to sell furniture, stationery, and fancy groceries. Before he knew it, R. H. Macy had a department store and was doing a thriving business.

Macy's idea now was to provide everything a customer could possibly desire, and he tried to do just that. He directed his appeal to women shoppers, who, by definition, are bargain hunters, and he wooed the patronage of the many by a large variety of merchandise in twenty-two different departments, each with its own buyer. Stewart's and Field's might cater to the classes, but R. H. Macy's was for the masses, the female masses.

By the time its founder died in Paris in 1877, Macy's was selling over a million dollars' worth of goods a year. When the store moved to its present location on Herald Square at Thirty-fourth Street in 1902, it was doing an annual business of more than ten million dollars. Like Stewart, Wanamaker, and Field, Macy sold each article at one fixed price. He sold sound articles, but he sold for cash, and he sold good value for fair price. Instead of the elegance of Field's or Wanamaker's, he eschewed decor for the sake of economy and to give the impression of economy.

Macy's is a block-long bargain basement on many floors. Its reiterated promise is that it tries to sell everything for 6 percent less for cash. Though it handles expensive as well as cheaper merchandise, it competes vigorously through its loudly advertised policy of selling for less. Known the world over, Macy's means bigness, variety, economy, repeated sales, standard merchandise, and merchandise which it has manufactured to its specifications and then sells under its own brand names. Modern Macy's, with about seventy departments stocking some 400,000 items, serves over 150,000 shoppers every day. Macy's is as much New York as the city's subways and skyscrapers.

As the world knows, for it is told so every year, Christmas belongs to Macy's. The store declares this with blaring bands, huge balloons, and in living color with its annual toy parade on Thanksgiving. Nationally televised, the parade brings the one and only Macy's Santa Claus to town like the V.I.P. he is, and the Christmas shopping season is formally opened once again.

The merchant princes of the nineteenth century, with their residential palaces and retail emporia, were folk heroes of that era. They were marketing entrepreneurs, self-made men who achieved success and great wealth on what was then the approved American pattern. They were the great men in the famous novels of Horatio Alger, Jr. When his rags-to-riches hero stopped a runaway horse and rescued the helpless heroine, she was usually the daughter of a great merchant who rewarded the hero with a job in his countinghouse. The poor but honest boy then married the heiress and rose to become a merchant prince himself, with his own coach, mansion, and country estate.

These men were—and their successors with their mammoth organizations are—at one end, the consumer end, of the marketing process. Department stores buy what they do not make, in many markets and in many different ways. Between them and the shoppers they serve, there is a long and often intricate marketing operation. It varies from product to product and from company to company, and it is always changing. Yet there are basic parts of the overall marketing process that are roughly fixed and affect many and disparate products.

— 4 —

Pricing and Packaging for the Market

Marketing begins long before any finished product is made for distribution and sale to the consumer. Raw materials come from the farm, the forest, and the mine, even from the chemical laboratory—foods, wood, metals, chemicals. These must be obtained from the earth, processed, and marketed to producers of industrial and consumer goods. Often they do not go straight to these producers but pass through the hands of several buyers, agents, brokers, jobbers, and wholesalers.

Suppose a man raises sunflowers for the market. He must first obtain seed from a seedsman who has raised and cultivated sunflowers to produce fertile seed and usually experimented with several varieties over a period of years to develop a productive strain for *his* market. The grower then plows, harrows, fertilizes, and plants the ground, buying the equipment he must use in the agricultural implement market and expending his own time and labor. He tends the growing plants, cultivates, weeds, protects his tall bright yellow flowers from wind, weather, and birds. In a good season, and he does not always have one, he grows a rich crop ready for harvesting.

The sunflowers may be bought while still standing in the field, or the harvested flowers may be purchased by a man or organization that extracts the seeds, dries them, and markets them to wholesalers who store and transport them to *their* markets. These buyers may be florists, seedsmen, makers of salad oil and margarine, soap, protein-rich cattle cake, or packagers of wild bird feed. These buyers and producers in turn market their sunflower seeds or items made from them to the ultimate consumer. The sunflower has many uses. In some parts of the world it is used for human food. Its stalks and leaves make good silage. Ash from the stems of the plant is high in potassium. It is used as a fertilizer and sometimes in glassmaking.

The ordinary sunflower then may go into any of these markets and change hands a dozen times. The consumer may be an industry which uses it to make other things or an individual consumer who buys what the grower has raised in the form of edible oils, vegetable lard, or bagged seeds from his local grocer or produce market.

The sunflower seed provides a simple example of comparatively simple marketing. The marketing progression is much more complicated for some other products, say, for the materials and component parts which go into the manufacture of an automobile.

Nuts and bolts don't grow on trees or spring out of the ground. They are made. You can begin with the iron ore, which must be refined, then sold to steel makers who sell to foundries who sell to machine shops. The shops may belong to the automotive manufacturer, who fashions the nuts and bolts to the sizes and tolerances he requires, or to independent nuts and bolts manufacturers who sell to the automotive manufacturers. You can trace marketing back even farther—to the industrial sand which must be quarried, then marketed and transported to the foundries which make the dies and castings from which engine blocks and other component parts of automobiles are assembled. Nothing comes from nothing, and tools and machinery have to be made before they can be used to make new tools and machines.

There is marketing from the very beginning, but the marketing with which most of us are concerned is that which begins with a product's being canned, quick-frozen, sewed, molded, bottled, manufactured, or somehow concocted in a plant or a number of plants for the consumer market.

Suppose you decide to make and sell clothespins. You have the factory, the necessary machinery, the executive and sales personnel, and a dependable labor supply. You have, or know where you can obtain, the necessary wood to transform into clothespins. You find out that you should be able to make them for so much a gross or a freight-car load.

You know—or you had better know—where you are going to market them. Perhaps a large wholesaler has let it be known that he is in the market for so many million clothespins. A retail chain may be shopping for them. You may have explored the market for yourself and discovered how many clothespins the average household uses in a year, how many families use electric dryers, and how many hang their washing to dry outdoors on clear days and in the basement or attic when it rains.

Now you have choices to make. You can make your clothespins out of good hardwood, say, maple or birch. You can go to the other extreme and use the cheapest woods you can buy. If you wish to stay in the clothespin market, you will probably use good hardwood that still is not good enough for fine furniture or the interior trim of a house. If you just want to make a quick killing, then get out of the market; it does not matter whether the pins split when they are first forced over a clothesline or splinter in the housewives' hands By that time you will be making rake handles or picnic tables or have retired on your clothespin fortune.

If you decide to make good clothespins, the difference in cost will be the quality of the wood, for the manufacturing process will be much the same and will take the same machinery and labor time. There may be another substantial expense. You may decide to sell your clothespins as branded products in the national market. This means advertising, frequent and continuous, to convince the housewife that your clothespins are better than those of any other brand and infinitely better than any unbranded clothespins.

All of this you will have to decide before you make one clothespin, and many manufacturers—as witness the frequency of business failure—make the wrong decisions. There are other risks. Everyone may decide to use gas or electric dryers, or the government, urged on by the competition, may declare outdoor drying on clotheslines illegal. People may suddenly decide that plastic clothespins are superior to wood. For that matter, they may decide to wear only disposable clothes or even to wear no clothes at all. Marketing would be much simpler if the consumer were predictable. He seldom is.

You gauge the possibilities and weigh the risks as best you can and decide to go ahead. You start production, pay your overhead, pay your workers, perhaps borrow large sums from banks or sell stock in your enterprise. You make a million or a billion clothespins. What now?

You know, or your cost accountant can figure out, how much it has cost to make the clothespins by the gross, the hundred, or whatever quantity you use as base. You know how much profit you wish to make or must make. Then you set a price to the wholesaler, another to chain or very large retailers who buy directly from you (these prices are sometimes the same), and another to smaller independent purchasers. In other words, you price your product to your market with the cost, the prices charged by other clothespin manufacturers, and the customary retail price in mind.

Pricing is always difficult for the marketer. He can seldom be sure that he has set his price correctly. It may be too high or too low. The best he can do is use one or a combination of several tested methods.

The manufacturer may set a price on what he makes which he knows from experience or investigation will cover his costs and return him a reasonable profit. He may set a high profit percentage on large items of infrequent purchase or a small percentage on less expensive items which are quickly used and must be replaced. Generally, profit margins are high on durable and semidurable goods (automobiles, furniture, major household appliances) and low on goods, like foods, which are bought often and quickly consumed, so that there is an almost immediate resale market. Pricing in this way is known as cost-plus pricing.

Though it has almost been outmoded by government controls, regulations, and subsidies, the law of supply and demand has never been repealed. If you have and wish to sell what someone else desperately desires, you can charge him as much as your conscience will allow—and usually it will allow a good deal. If you had the only golf ball available for a professional tournament, you could sell it for almost the $30,000 or $100,000 prize money. Corner the total supply of gold, feathers, or moonbeams, and you can name your own price. When demand outruns supply, the marketer can safely ask a high price. When there is no demand for his typewriters, plastic hoes, gold-plated wheelbarrows, or whatever it is, it does not matter what price he asks. He will not get it. A balance between supply and demand, which is the more usual situation, means that the marketer can set an equitable price which allows him a fair margin of profit and that he can be fairly sure of steady sales.

Some manufacturers use the break-even point in pricing. This means that you can make and sell so many of a product and recover your costs. The price you set will bring back the money you spent in production after you have successfully marketed a certain number. You make and sell 5,000 gross of fishhooks. That is your break-even point. Your plant is already tooled. Your salesmen are on the road, and your workers know their jobs. The next 5,000 or 5,000,000 gross you sell represent pure profit except for your overhead.

This system is used in businesses such as the printing of

magazines. The principal manufacturing cost is in typesetting, composition, plating, and make-ready on the press. Once the presses start rolling, it is as easy to run off 10,000,000 copies as 5,000,000. The first few thousand may cost you one dollar a copy to print, the next few somewhat less, and the last million practically nothing. The mass magazine publisher knows from experience that if he sells a certain number, perhaps 2,000,000 copies, he has reached his break-even point. He has made no profit on those. He begins to make a profit with copy number 2,000,001.

In pricing, a manufacturer has to be guided in part by what his competition charges for the same product. Call $3,000 the average list price of a medium-priced automobile. If the competitor charges that amount, you must charge about the same for a comparable car. If you can make and sell it for $2,995, you will have a price advantage. If, instead, you can convince the consumer through advertising that your car is worth that much more, you may be able to list yours at $3,495. Your car may well be worth the difference, but it does not have to be. The value has to be in the mind of the purchaser, not necessarily in the automobile.

There are, or were until inflation made values meaningless, traditional retail prices or price ranges in many lines. Except for state and local taxes, a candy bar was long sold for five or ten cents. Through huge-quantity purchases direct from the manufacturers, some outlets could market nickel bars at three for a dime. Popular brands of cigarettes sold for many years at fifteen cents a pack. Punitive taxation intended by reformers to act as a restraint—and at the same time swell government funds —has more than tripled the price in many states.

A packet of English lavender seed has always sold for twenty-five or thirty cents at retail. That is what amateur gardeners are used to paying. The marketer of the seeds must price them so that retailers can sell them for about that price. If he finds that is too little for him to make a profit, he can put less seed or poorer seed into the envelope and tell the consumer that it is more and better. It will be at least a year and a half before the buyer can find out whether or not he was misled, and by that time he may have forgotten whose brand of seed he used, or may have transferred his attention from lavender to hyssop. Germination, only about 10 percent, is low for lavender anyway, so the distributor has that much protection.

Once a product has been priced, it has to be packaged, and the package is one of the most important considerations in modern marketing. Go back to the clothespins. Put a dozen in a flat cardboard or plastic box with a transparent top so that the shopper can see them lying in a row like tin soldiers, and they may look so attractive that the housewife is persuaded to buy and may not even demur at paying a premium for their handsome appearance. Instead, wire a bundle of sturdy-looking pins together and their appearance may convince of their durability. Throw them loose in a paper bag and they look undistinguished, not good enough for hanging the best sheets, a delicate blouse, or a drip-dry shirt on the line.

In consumer goods the package is part of the marketing effort. It must protect its contents, be distinctive, attract attention, arouse approval, and lead to such familiarity that it will be instantly recognizable anywhere. This is particularly important in self-service outlets where there is no salesman or saleswoman to call attention to a brand. Campbell's Soup, Uneeda Biscuits, Morton's Salt, Ivory Soap, Quaker Oats, Beechnut Chewing Gum, and scores of other branded products come readily to mind as familiar packages. There are many others. The Hershey chocolate company to 1971 had never used print or electronic advertising, but Hershey's has always advertised. Its brown wrapper with the familiar silver lettering is the best possible advertising for that favored product.

Once a package has been designed, used, and become known, the wise manufacturer hesitates to change it except in unnoticeable detail. A few years ago the makers and distributors of a popular brand of cigarettes decided to give their package a clean, contemporary look and did. Aesthetically the new package was pleasing, but smokers of the brand would have none of it. This did not look like the cigarette they preferred. They suspected it was not the same. The company hastily went back to using its old package. A well-known brand of cough drops had the same experience and retreated to using the bearded brothers on the old-fashioned package.

The design of an automobile, its styling and appearance, is merely the package for an engine, four wheels, and the promise of pride, pleasure, and speed. In part, the design is functional, but its real purpose is to enhance the desirability of the car. Though they may do it with varying degrees of comfort and convenience, the Rolls Royce or the Lincoln Continental perform exactly the same function as the Toyota or the Aston Martin. The package into which one car puts its mobility says luxury, ease, and comfort; that of another, economy; that of another, unlimited speed and rakish daring. The Rolls Royce could easily change its packaging, but the Rolls of today looks basically like the Rolls of the 1920's, and the Volkswagen of any year looks just like the Volkswagen of any other year. Other automobile manufacturers deliberately change the appearance of their cars each year in order to make their older models look antiquated and in need of replacement, but they have learned—as Chrysler did when it introduced its streamlined models in the 1930's—that they must not change them too much. Startling innovations in appearance disconcert, and the car-buying public will not accept them. An automobile manufacturer has a bad year when people decide that they do not like a car's appearance. The car may have mechanical improvements of many kinds, added speed and economy of operation, an assortment of spellbinding accessories, but if people do not recognize or like the package, they will not buy its contents.

After the product, clothespin or car, has been planned and designed for the market, priced and packaged for the market, one more fundamental marketing operation must be performed. This is distribution. Physically, this is the movement of goods through various channels from point of production to a market or many markets where they will be placed on sale. It is both the transfer of goods, with several changes of hands en route, and the transfer of ownership from original producer and marketer to the ultimate buyer.

— 5 —

Marketing Channels

Without any effort at all, on almost any main highway in the United States, you can get behind a huge trailer truck or two or six in a line, or get sandwiched between two of them, or find one of the monsters breathing down your neck at eighty miles per hour. You can decide whether it is better to go ninety yourself and get away from it or slow down to forty and hope it will pass without swamping your car in the back draft or—it seems the wisest move—get off the highway.

These mammoth trucks are taking goods to market. The one behind you may be loaded with business-machine parts and the one following with live chickens. A tremendous tanker may be carrying gasoline, molasses, milk, or chemicals. Foodstuffs, clothing, cereals, aspirin, cigarettes, liquor, and costume jewelry, destined for different purchasers, may all be riding in one truck. Another may contain only eggs, explosives, or candy. You can seldom tell from seeing the behemoth blur past what is in it, but usually the cargo is worth many thousands, perhaps hundreds of thousands of dollars. It is this that makes hijacking prevalent and profitable, and large-scale marketing possible.

The trucks you see may belong to a manufacturer, a large wholesaler, a department store, a grocery, drug, or variety chain, or to a trucking fleet working for any of them. Whichever they are, they are moving goods. Trains for the movement of people are disappearing as fast as the railroads can get government permission to get out of the passenger-hauling business, but the more profitable movement of inanimate cargo by railway freight goes on. Wheat reaches the grain elevators of cereal manufacturers, rags the papermaker, refrigerated foods the vegetable and fruit wholesalers and then the produce markets by railway freight. New automobiles go overland either on double-decker truck carriers or piggyback on long lines of flatcars. Over the highways or down the tracks, to market, to market they go.

These trucks and freights are performing an economic service. City dwellers do not need to find a farm and interview a hen in order to purchase an egg. Eggs have been transported to the grocery store. People do not have to raise and slaughter a cow or steer to get a steak or a side of beef. The meat is in from Chicago or Omaha—or the Argentine. A man does not have to go to Detroit or its environs to buy a new car. His local dealer has a selection. Transportation is a physical marketing service which adds to the value of a product, any product except one grown or made in the neighborhood. In every case the consumer pays for that service, just as he pays for the services of a doctor or a lawyer. Usually about 15 percent of the purchase price to the consumer is for transportation to market.

The actual transport of marketed products is something you can see. The consumer is also paying for other services involved in the transfer of goods from the producer to him which he cannot see but which are just as necessary in marketing.

Goods may move directly from producer to consumer, that is, from factory to home. These are sold by the house-to-house salesmen of the manufacturer. Brushes, cosmetics, stockings, and household products are sold in this way. Goods ordered from mail-order catalogs go directly to the consumer, who must pay the ever-increasing postal charges. Only a small percentage of products sold go directly to the consumer in these ways.

Frozen-food packers who grow their own produce may sell directly to retail outlets. Quantity retail buyers who purchase or contract for the output of entire factories or operate their own plants obtain some of their products directly. Automobile manufacturers send their new cars and trucks directly from their assembly lines to retail dealers who, as they are franchised by the manufacturers, are, in effect, manufacturers' agents even when they conduct independent retail businesses. This is producer-to-retailer distribution.

In the more usual marketing process, goods and products move from the maker to a wholesaler, then to a retailer, finally to the consumer. A vital product illustrates this movement on a vast scale.

Surpassed only by agriculture and the public utilities—gas, electricity, and communications combined—the petroleum industry is the third largest in the United States. The country's oil companies have about $80 billion in fixed assets here and over $32 billion abroad. About 3.2 billion barrels of crude oil are produced annually from more than 583,000 oil wells in the United States.

This oil must be transported from the fields in western Texas, the midcontinent, Alaska, and offshore drillings to the refineries. The largest oil refineries in the world are along the Texas and Louisiana coasts. The three next largest in the United States are in the Philadelphia, Los Angeles, and Chicago areas. There are other important refining centers near New York, St. Louis, San Francisco, and Seattle. In all, the petroleum industry has about 275 operating refineries. Crude oil enters them and emerges as product oil—gasoline, kerosine, diesel fuel, home-heating oil, and other petroleum products like liquefied petroleum gas and asphalt.

Just as the crude oil is transported to the refineries, the product oil must be transported from them to market. Oil moves through great pipelines, goes by ocean tankers, by barges along inland waterways, by railroad tank cars, and by tank trucks. In the United States there are 217,000 miles of petroleum and gas pipelines, up to thirty-six inches in diameter, transporting gasoline and other forms of liquid energy as well as crude oil to points up to a thousand miles away. There are 81,000 tank cars; 158,000 tank trucks; 387 ocean tankers; 2,800 barges. These figures give some idea of the massive transport involved.

All of this petroleum flows through wholesalers. There are about 40,000 independent companies engaged in the production, refining, transportation, and wholesale distribution of petroleum. Gasoline and home-heating oil go to some 12,000 wholesalers who operate about 30,000 bulk plants and terminals. Gasoline is marketed from these wholesalers and their storage facilities to more than 219,000 service stations.

As the petroleum industry likes to point out, there is an oddity about the distribution of gasoline and oil. No one ever sees it. It is piped from wells far below the earth's surface to flow at about three miles an hour to the refineries or slosh along in tank ships, barges, freight tankers, or trucks. It is out of sight in bulk storage plants and in the underground tanks of retail service stations. Then it is poured through a hose into the tanks of cars or the tanks of houses that are heated by oil. No one sees it, but we would soon know if the fuel were not there. Generating plants which use fuel oil would be stilled; cars, trucks, and buses would not go; and a few million homes would be cold.

The gallon of gasoline that the motorist has put into his car has come a long way: from Texas, Alaska, perhaps Saudi Arabia. It is marketed through wholesalers and retailers in a highly competitive business. The major oil companies advertise strongly and continuously. They sell the same gasoline, but each company has changed it by the kinds and amounts of additives inserted to give its brand its advertised virtues.

There are more people, about 840,600 of them, engaged in the marketing of gasoline, heating oil, and other petroleum products than in oil field production, refining, and pipeline operations combined.

There has always been oil. It has lain underground for geologic ages. Men have been getting it out since Edwin L. Drake drilled the first successful well in Titusville, Pennsylvania, in August, 1859. The complex and difficult part of the operation is getting the refined product to industrial and individual users at a low price per gallon and at a profit to the many companies which in one way or another employ 1.2 million in the petroleum industry.

Another basic industry depends upon the wholesaler in its marketing.

By estimate of the American Forest Institute, some 3,200 billion board feet of lumber have been produced and used in this country. Yet there is still enough sawtimber in the forests of the United States to build a six-room house for every man, woman, and child in the country. Intensive methods of tree farming—trees grown as a crop—add continually to the supply.

Harvested timber goes to the sawmills, then to about four thousand wholesale lumber dealers. From them it goes directly to industry or to about thirty thousand retail lumberyards and from them to builders and householders. Wood products such as pulpwood, hardboards, even the rayon used in textiles and in automobile tire fabric, reach the consumer through other wholesale and retail markets. The manufacture and marketing of lumber and wood products (furniture excepted) accounts for about 4.5 percent of the national income of the United States.

Most other kinds of goods and products also move through wholesale channels. The wholesaler buys in large lots and sells in smaller lots. He buys at manufacturers' prices, with discounts from them for quantity purchase and prompt payment, and sells to retailers at prices that enable him to make a profit. He maintains warehouses which otherwise the manufacturer would have to maintain. He employs a sales force, often a large one, to call on the retail trade. He is responsible for transportation from the point of product origin to the retailer. He provides credit to the retailer which otherwise the manufacturer would have to extend, thus saving the manufacturer bookkeeping and credit risk. The wholesaler can push a manufacturer's brand in competition with other nationally advertised brands, private brands, and unbranded merchandise in the same line.

The wholesaler does these and other things for the manufacturer. He does as much for the retailer. He keeps him supplied with products the retailer's customers will buy. He knows from previous orders and the retailer's sales records what products and what brands of those products are moving and which are staying on the store shelves. In this way the wholesaler can and does help with the retailer's inventory. He can advise on brand selection or on how to move slow-moving items. Like the manufacturer, the wholesaler can give discounts on quantity orders and offer attractive deals on merchandise that is in large supply. His extension of credit to the retailer is even more important in marketing than the manufacturer's extension of credits to him.

Perhaps most important of all, the wholesaler stocks the products of many manufacturers. The wholesaler is a central point of supply for the retailer, who thus does not have to order from many makers, some at a great distance, and suffer expensive delay and complicated record keeping. The retailer might not even be able to purchase some items directly, as many manufacturers refuse to fill small orders, to "drop ship," as it is called, because it is too time-consuming and expensive.

Bargain houses sometimes claim they can sell cheaper because they have "eliminated the middleman." This is a catch phrase which seldom means much. Elimination of the middleman does not always mean lower prices to the consumer.

If a retailer decides to do his own wholesaling, he must himself do the distribution, warehousing, selling, and transportation. He must establish his own wholesaling organization, maintain his own storehouses, arrange and finance his own transportation, and all the rest. Because he is skilled at retailing does not mean that he is skilled at wholesaling. He is apt to be less efficient and economical than the professional wholesaler. In the end, the savings to the consumer may be nil. The consumer price may well be more than if the product had gone through established wholesaling channels.

The same is true for manufacturing. A large retailer may decide to make his own automobile tires or pantyhose and sell them directly to the public. Elimination of all the work and people between production and final sale should give him a cheaper product which he can market more cheaply and at a higher price. The trouble this time is that retailers are not manufacturers. They may be able to hire production experts, rent or build efficient plants, engage capable managers and skilled craftsmen. Then, again, they may not. The manufacturing retailer may well not be able to meet the competition from established manufacturers of tires or pantyhose who can undersell him with better products to his retail rivals. Retailers have sometimes gone into wholesaling or manufacturing, or both, with happy enthusiasm, then escaped from them with wild relief.

The importance of wholesalers in marketing is manifested by their number and by the volume of business that they handle. In 1958 there were 285,043 wholesale establishments in the United States. Five years later, in 1963, the number had risen to 308,177. These wholesalers in many lines—groceries, apparel, tobacco, liquor, electrical goods, paper, furniture, and many other products—employed 3,088,706 men and women, and their sales in that year, the latest for which complete figures are available, totaled $157,392,000,000, which is a considerable amount of money. Undoubtedly all of these figures are larger now.

Methods of marketing may vary from this manufacturer-wholesaler-retailer-consumer pattern. They vary from product to product and maker to maker. An industry or a producer within an industry may use a combination of all the methods just discussed.

This book or any book can serve as an example of the dual

marketing of a product: the primary marketing of the elements that are used to make the product, then the marketing of the finished book to the reader.

A book is a simple physical object which you can see, feel, sometimes even smell. It is made of paper, printer's ink, a binding of paper, buckram, leather, or some synthetic substance over boards, thread, and glue. All of the elements must be assembled from many markets. Pulpwood must be produced and sold to the papermaker and ink to the printer. Type must be made in some foundry for the monotype or linotype machines which have been built for the printing trade. The stereotyper and the plate maker must draw on raw materials, tools, and machines from many sources. The binder must obtain his supplies. The book provides a market for many products even before it exists.

To make it exist, a writer spends months or years in research, travel, study. He buys a typewriter, paper, pens, pencils—and erasers. A publisher agrees to risk issuing what the writer writes in book form, undertaking to do this only if he believes he can market enough copies to make a profit. He spends his money for editing, typesetting, press work, binding, shipping, and all the other operations entailed.

The publisher sets a list price on the book that he believes will pay its costs and return him a profit. He then sells copies of the book at approximately half this list price to a giant wholesaler who handles the books of many publishers. In turn, the wholesaler markets the book at a somewhat higher price to retail book stores or the book departments of department stores, and they market it to the reader at the list price. The publisher also often sells directly to the retailer, bypassing the wholesaler, and infrequently, directly to the consumer.

Manufacturers do not release cost and profit figures. These are closely guarded business secrets. Sometimes when a company makes an entire line of products, it actually does not know the cost of one of them, only its complete production costs and what income it has made or failed to make on its entire output. Privately owned companies do not have to issue any profit and loss statement. Only companies in which shares are owned by the general public are obliged by law to publish annual reports. Thus, actual cost and profit data for any company, when not impossible to obtain, are data hard to come by.

What is certain is that the consumer pays, in general, about twice the original cost of a product. He seldom pays less. He often pays more, much more. After an exhaustive study, *Does Distribution Cost Too Much?* published in 1939, the Twentieth Century Fund came to the conclusion that distribution, that is, marketing, accounts for fifty-nine cents of the consumer dollar and production for forty-one cents. Marketing a product costs more than making it.

The difference is not all profit to anyone. A complexity of costs are involved, and many operations are performed between the point of origin and the point of sale. All must be paid for.

With a book, the product marketing is about like this. The publisher sets a list price of, say, $5.00 a copy. Depending upon quality of paper, printing, binding, and whether or not it is illustrated, the book has cost him anywhere from perhaps thirty-nine cents to about eighty cents a copy to produce. He sells copies to the book wholesaler at about 50 to 55 percent off list, that is for $2.50 or $2.25 each. The retailer obtains his copies from the wholesaler at from 40 to 46 percent off the list price. He then sell copies at the published price of $5.00.

In this instance the largest share of the profit goes to the publisher, who usually pays the writer 10 percent of list price, less on quantity sales and on sales at higher-than-usual discounts. The bookseller makes at least $2.00 on every single copy sale. He, of course, has to pay his rent, his lighting, his help, and his taxes. The book may sell well, in which case the publisher realizes a handsome profit (which he may lose on other books), or it may not sell at all, in which case the publisher realizes a handsome loss. Booksellers who have bought on approval may return unsold copies. The publisher then remainders the edition by selling the books at cost or less to cheap outlets, or, as the phrase is, sends them to the choppers—in other words, junks them for the small value of the used paper.

All kinds of variations are possible even here. If the book is successful, the publisher can run off cheaper editions using the same plates. He can issue it or sell the rights for its issuance in paperback form. A large publisher can promote the book through his own retail outlets, use it as a give-away premium in book-club offers, or offer it free with magazine subscriptions. Sometimes the best that publisher (and writer) can do when a book has failed to find a market is to forget the whole thing— or try to. That is exactly what producers in other lines are sometimes forced to do.

The proportion of the retail price of an object that goes to pay for distribution and what part of the price that goes to its makers and its various handlers varies from product to product. The farmer who raises the fruits and vegetables gets a very small part of the consumer dollar spent for canned goods. Most of it goes to the canner. The factory and the wholesaler make far less on the sale of a refrigerator or a television set than the retailer. About half the price of the major appliance stays with him.

It is the processors who get by far the greatest share in cereals. Dewhurst and Stewart in *Does Distribution Cost Too Much?* commented that bread and cereals both sell at retail prices which are anywhere from 143 to 975 percent higher than the farm value of the grain from which they are made. The prices of bread and cereals have at least tripled since they wrote, but there is little reason to suspect that the farmer is taking more or the processor less.

It is, in general, a matter of low volume and high markup or high volume and low markup, as in grocery products, where the percentage of profit per item to the retailer is low to very low. Meat prices are high enough to raise buyer protests and for housewives in some communities to organize boycotts. Most of the consumer dollar here goes to the packer, who must transport and slaughter the animals, and to the wholesaler, who stores and ships the dressed carcasses, but with small profit to either. About 20 percent of the consumer's meat dollar goes to retailers, who must pay their overhead and their meatcutters. The cattle rancher and the feeder make less per head of cattle than they did twenty years ago. Though their operation is highly efficient, the packers are said to be making only a 2 percent profit, and the meat departments of chain stores only about 2 percent before taxes. The tremendous increase in meat prices, as with many other products, seems to be due to increased labor costs all down the line: in trucking, slaughtering, and meat cutting. Inflation produced by these causes is behind what seems the unconscionable rise in the retail price of beef.

Not distribution costs but high markups account for high prices in luxury merchandise. The traditional retail markup on jewelry is 100 percent, and it is often more. People do not buy jewelry that often. The sale of a piece of real jewelry must repay the jeweler for his original investment, his safekeeping, often for a long time, and his display. When jewelry is sold on the installment plan, the first payment usually covers the cost. It may often include a profit. Later payments simply add to the profit.

Marketing as distribution in all of its aspects adds to the cost of products to the consumer. It also adds appreciably to the value of what he buys. The steak, macadamia nuts, computer, or yacht has to be available when he wishes it where he wants it, and where it is so displayed that the consumer has a choice. Marketing gets it there.

— 6 —

Marketing of Automobiles

It is a debatable point whether Americans own automobiles or whether automobiles own the United States. The automobile has made and unmade cities. It has built millions of miles of paved highway and superhighway across prairies, under, over, or around mountains, and below the waters of rivers and harbors. It has moved shopping centers into the country and developed towns around them. It has destroyed railroads and built huge factories beyond the reach of public transportation. Trolley cars which could carry a hundred or more people to and from work or play have virtually disappeared. Bus lines have begged off running in many cities. One man or woman, or, if the driver cares to crowd his car, two, drive to work, to shop, to games, sometimes even home, in their personal tons of glass, metal, and rubber.

Automotive manufacturers build and sell about 9 million new passenger cars every year and more than 1.7 million trucks and buses, their total value at factory prices running over $21 billion. There are nearly 80 million passenger cars registered in the United States—nearly 100 million automotive vehicles on the road. Many families have two cars; some have three or even four. The American lives with, in, and often for his automobile.

One United States business in every six is automotive. Dealers

64

in cars and accessories, and gasoline service stations do 17.5 percent of all retail business. Wholesalers of cars, equipment, and fuel do nearly 20 percent of wholesale business; garages and repair points, motels and tourist courts make up 18 percent of all wholesale and retail sales. The automotive industry is a vast complex whose tentacles writhe through the entire United States economy.

Besides all the original and directly connected activities, the industry indirectly supports, or helps to support, many other industries engaged in producing the raw materials that go into cars and trucks and original or replacement parts. Road builders, the builders of machinery for them, bridge builders, cement producers, quarry workers, and scores of others are dependent upon the automobile for most of their business. Thousands of retail outlets in shopping centers across the country could not exist without the automobile which, in most cases, is the only way customers have of reaching the stores.

You can argue the question whether Americans own cars or cars own them, but if you take the first stand you will lose. The automobile has changed American life fundamentally, and increased the tempo of living from six or eight miles per hour to somewhere about eighty miles per hour with no indication that the limit has been reached.

From the very beginning of its comparatively short history, marketing has been as important as production in wreaking the changes—for good, evil, or, as with most things, something of each—that the automobile has wrought.

In 1892, two brothers, Charles E. and J. Frank Duryea, bought a secondhand buggy, a phaeton really, but no horse. They intended to make their phaeton horseless. Charles Duryea, who was making bicycles in Peoria, Illinois, did most of the design of the vehicle which he and his brother hoped would propel itself, then he went back to Peoria. J. Frank Duryea, a mechanic at the Ames Manufacturing Company in Chicopee, Massachusetts, went to work with the help of Erwin

F. Markham to build it in the machine shop of W. J. Taylor & Sons in nearby Springfield. They built a one-cylinder gasoline engine, devised their own ignition system, and concocted a carburetor out of a perfume atomizer and an alcohol burner.

After working and tinkering for more than a year, they waited until after dark the night of September 21, 1893, to harness a horse to their contraption and tow it to the home of Markham's son-in-law on a residential street in Springfield. They dismissed the horse and the next morning managed to start their motorized phaeton. It spluttered, coughed, then took hold and chugged rhythmically. J. Frank Duryea climbed in, took the steering tiller, and bumped down the street on the first trial run of the first American automobile.

Duryea made indicated changes in the clutch and transmission, then took the car for a half-mile run in November. So successful was this that the Duryeas founded the Duryea Motor Wagon Company in Springfield in January, 1894, and went into production of "Motor Wagons, Motors, and Automobile Vehicles of All kinds." The quotation is from their first advertisement; its illustration showed two women, one driving, the other a passenger in a Duryea. The automobile industry began its marketing appeal to women almost as soon as it was born.

Another and more spectacular kind of automobile advertising began almost as early and continues in roaring splendor. The Indianapolis 500 and all the other automobile races are not only tests of cars, fuels, tracks, and human daring and endurance, but also magnificent advertising for every automotive item used.

J. Frank Duryea built a two-cylinder car which he named the Buggyaut and entered a race sponsored by the Chicago *Times-Herald*. Nearly a hundred cars were entered for the race held on Thanksgiving Day in 1895, but only six made the starting line. There were three Benz cars made in Europe, two electrics, and the Buggyaut. The race was from Chicago to Evanston and back, a distance of fifty-four miles. It was cold and windy. Snow from a blizzard lay on the ground. An umpire rode with each driver, and Charles Duryea came up from Peoria to watch his brother race.

Marveling crowds lined the course. The two electrics burned out their batteries before they got out of Chicago. The Benz sponsored by R. H. Macy collided with a horsecar. A French driver in another Benz was forced out when his solid-rubber tires spun in the snow. The driver of the third Benz became exhausted by the cold. A replacement took over, but he lost consciousness at Fifty-fifth and Halsted in Chicago on the return, and the umpire with him had to grasp the controls. This was the only other car to cross the finish line. J. Frank Duryea and his Buggyaut lost fifty-five minutes at one point when Duryea had to repair his steering gear and enlist the help of an astounded tinsmith, who was eating his Thanksgiving dinner, to help repair the sparker, but the Buggyaut won. It covered the fifty-four miles in seven hours and fifty-three minutes.

The $2,000 prize enabled the Duryeas to make more of their motor wagons. They entered four of them in a race from City Hall in New York to Irvington-on-the-Hudson and back, beat a field of foreign cars, and won another $3,000. This capital went to making a total of twelve Duryea motor wagons in 1896. Two were sent to England, where J. Frank Duryea drove one against forty-odd steam, electric, and gasoline-driven cars in a race from London to Brighton on November 14, 1896. This was the Emancipation Race, held to celebrate repeal of the English law which ordered that a "road locomotive" had to be preceded by a man bearing a red flag. Duryea was among the last to start but came in an hour ahead of the car which placed second.

The Duryeas were running advertisements—one was in the first issue of *The Horseless Age*—and winning races, but their greatest publicity came from another source.

Barnum & Bailey's Greatest Show on Earth opened in Madison Square Garden in 1896 with a Duryea as the featured exhibit. It was billed as: "The famous Duryea Motor Wagon, or

Motorcycle, the identical HORSELESS CARRIAGE that won the great race in Chicago last November." Everywhere the Barnum & Bailey show went, the Duryea was driven in circus parades. It was put through its paces in the big top as part of the entertainment. Huge crowds gawked or were struck dumb with wonder. It goes by itself! Look! No horse!

Car fever gripped other bicycle makers and mechanics. Elwood G. Haynes designed and drove his first car (it was made by Edgar and Elmer Apperson) in Kokomo, Indiana, on July 4, 1894. Henry Ford, who had been a watch repairman, then an engineer with the Edison Illuminating Company, built and drove his first car in Detroit in 1896, but Charles Brady King drove the first automobile in that city, a high delivery wagon with a gasoline engine. Alexander Winton built his first car in Cleveland in 1896.

The human being seems to have an inborn love of locomotion, the faster, the better. A hobby horse, a sled, a ride on or behind a horse was a delight. Here was something better than all of them. The public was entranced as the automobile tried to prove itself. Another race was on now, a scramble by designers, mechanics, and enthusiasts to get enough money to build cars for sale. Capital was not as enthusiastic. Who knew whether or not the new horseless carriage was anything but a toy? The craze might not last. Yet, in 1899, there were eighty companies making or getting ready to make automobiles—electric, steam, or internal combustion. F. O. and F. E. Stanley founded the Stanley Steam Car Company in Newton, Massachusetts, in 1897. R. E. Olds started the Olds Motor Vehicle Company in Detroit. The Autocar, Winton, Pullman, Cadillac, Locomobile, Austin, Elmore, Packard, Peerless, Pierce-Arrow, Franklin, Marmon, Studebaker, and White were all in production, and some were being mass-produced. Forty automotive manufacturers displayed their cars to 48,000 visitors to the first National Automobile Show held in Madison Square Garden in 1900.

The cars were smoky, noisy, and unreliable. Paved roads were virtually nonexistent. Roads were deep-rutted, dusty, or sloughs of mud. Early drivers were heroes. They had to withstand wind, weather, breakdowns, and the derision of bystanders. Frightened horses neighed and ran away. Enraged farmers cursed the new monsters. "Git a horse!" was the taunt when a car balked. "Get Out and Get Under" was a popular song.

People loved the automobile and hated it. Everybody wanted one, but they were expensive. The car became the symbol of wealth and the sporting proclivities of the idle rich. Much of the derision was born of envy. The first Vanderbilt Cup Race held on Long Island in 1904 was a social event as well as a competition among cars and drivers.

Cars were strongly advertised from the first. They had to be. The public had to be educated to the existence of a startling new product and persuaded to accept it. The automobile was exciting, but there were prejudices to break down. Moralists saw the automobile as somehow sinful, probably because it gave pleasure. Carriage makers, harness makers, horse traders, livery-stable owners, blacksmiths, and whip manufacturers feared damages to their businesses. They hated the automobile with, as Mark Twain said in talking of Yankee peddlers, a splendid energy. Towns passed stringent ordinances against the fire-eating dragons. In Minneapolis in 1902, a driver was arrested and fined ten dollars for breaking the ten-mile-an-hour speed limit.

Markets had to be established for the automobile, and there were major difficulties. Cars had not been perfected. Mechanical improvements of many kinds were still to be made. Product improvement is basic in the successful marketing of anything. Another handicap was fear. People used to traveling at a walk or the trot of a sedate horse had to be assured of the safety in traveling at speeds as high as twenty or thirty miles an hour.

The National Association of Automobile Manufacturers, which already had 112 members, adopted a sixty-day guarantee on new cars in 1902. This helped with car marketing, but price still remained a barrier to sales. A car cost more than a fairly good horse and carriage, and good old Dobbin could be counted on. Installment buying was the answer to the price problem.

It was not new. Cyrus Hall McCormick invented his Virginia Reaper in 1831, patented it in 1834, and began to exploit it a few years later. Manufacturing in Chicago, he convinced the farmer of the utility of his revolutionary machine, but it was costly. McCormick had his agents deliver the reaper to the farmer in the spring for a small down payment. The remainder of the price was not due until the farmer had reaped his fall crop.

The reaper was a productive tool for agricultural use, but the individual, notably the housewife, became familiar with installment buying through purchase of what quickly became a household necessity.

Isaac Singer, uneducated son of German immigrant parents, made his first sewing machine in Boston in 1850. He placed it on the market in competition with the machine made by Elias Howe, Jr. A "sewing machine war" ensued. After a compromise solution and consequent litigation, Singer began to sell his home sewing machines at about $125, a large sum of money in the 1850's. There was consumer resistance to the price, so in 1856 Singer began to deliver his sewing machines for five dollars down and the rest in monthly installments.

The usefulness of the machine, insistent salesmanship, and this ease of purchase placed Singer machines in thousands and thousands of homes around the world. By 1867, they were being manufactured in Glasgow, Scotland, as well as in the United States, and soon Singer sewing machines were being sold in Africa, Japan, Turkey, and many other countries. The Soviets seized more than $115 million worth of Singer property in Russia after World War One; after World War Two it stripped a Singer plant in Germany to set it up in Podolsk in the USSR. Its trademark the familiar red "S" with a woman at work on one of its machines, Singer sells many models today and conducts nearly two thousand sewing centers in the United States.

Installment selling had marketed a major farm machine and a domestic appliance. It could sell cars. Yet the automotive industry was incensed when Maxwell (forerunner of Chrysler) introduced the practice in 1905. Manufacturers needed capital, thus wanted their money. Again, moralists frowned. Installment buying was extravagance and would bring on all the evils that come with debt.

People proved that they would rather be debt-ridden than do without a car. Installment buying of automobiles has long been the rule rather than the exception. Most of the cars on the road are owned not by their occupants but by banks and finance companies. Cars are advertised with no full price mentioned, just a small down payment or no down payment at all, with thirty-six months to pay. Many people never own a car outright. They simply transfer installment payments from the old car to the new.

Car marketing helped to establish installment buying as the American way of life. As few can pay the total purchase price at once, people have long carried mortgages on their homes. Now many of the things in the houses are also being paid for as they are being used. Television sets, washers, dryers, refrigerators, ranges, even storm windows or a new bathroom can all be obtained for so much or so little down and the rest in regular installments. As a result, a large part of the family income may be ticketed for payment on this or that every time payday comes around.

The amounts of money owed banks and finance companies or the financing subdivisions of automotive companies increases each year. In 1940, outstanding consumer credit was little over $8.3 billion. By March, 1967, the figure had reached more than

$92.5 billion. When last counted, in March, 1969, total consumer credit stood at $119.95 billion with more than $89.672 billion of this amount owed for articles and services purchased on installment.

The other major force which broke the barrier of price in the marketing of automobiles was a man named Henry Ford.

Henry Ford built his first car in a shed behind his house. He ran it about a thousand miles, sold it for two hundred dollars, and built another one, which he ran around Detroit. As the Detroit Automobile Company, he began to build cars in 1899. The venture failed. He started the Henry Ford Automobile Company in 1902. It failed. Henry Ford then dropped everything else to build two tremendous racing cars, the Arrow and the 999. He sent to Salt Lake City for a famous bicycle racer, Barney Oldfield. In the 999, Oldfield won a three-mile race at Grosse Pointe, Michigan, by a half mile.

Barney Oldfield, who became even more famous as a racing driver than as a cyclist, and old 999, which had a 120-inch wheelbase, brought Henry Ford great national publicity. Always a shrewd salesman as well as a good mechanic, Ford capitalized on it. He formed the Ford Motor Company in June, 1903. He was its manager, superintendent, and master mechanic.

Ford began to manufacture both heavy and light cars and to advertise them even before he had one to sell. *The Saturday Evening Post* became and remained for a half century the showplace of automotive advertising. In the *Post* of June 27, 1903, eleven days after the Ford Motor Company had been organized, Ford pictured his proposed car as if it already existed: "BOSS OF THE ROAD . . . The Latest and the Best . . . Fordmobile with detachable tonneau $850." The Cadillac sold for the same price.

Ford hired top men as associates. Harold Wills, a bookkeeper for an adding-machine company, managed his shop and helped design the Ford car. Wills, who later made the big Wills–St.

Clair on his own, became Ford's chief engineer and production manager. Wills and Ford improved the Arrow racer and, with more newspaper fanfare, took it for speed trials on the ice of frozen Lake St. Clair.

Ford's advertising stressed the economy and durability of his lighter car. It boasted of the strong materials and sound workmanship. By 1905, Ford had a new plant on Piquette Avenue in Detroit with a huge sign over it reading: "The Home of the Celebrated Ford Automobile." All freight cars leaving the Ford plant bore big placards: "Loaded with Ford Automobiles."

Ford made 1,700 cars in 1903 and 1904. In 1906 and 1907 he made 8,423, nearly one-sixth of all the cars manufactured in the United States, and he marketed them strenuously. "Don't Experiment—Just Buy a Ford." Ford advertised the great size of his operation, and by 1907 the company devised the slogan it used for years: "Watch the Fords Go By."

Until 1908, Ford made both his light and his heavy car. Then he began to make only his "Universal Car." This was the wonderful, the legendary, the unforgettable Model T. It had the famous planetary transmission; three pedals—clutch, reverse, and brake. Its four-cylinder engine was under a black hood with a brass-topped radiator. Its high black body with its cloth top ran on four wooden-spoked wheels. This was the flivver, the tin lizzie, the jitney—the ugly, ungainly, inimitable Model T, which revolutionized the automotive industry and with it American life. In his first advertisement for it, Henry Ford made it clear that he knew what he was about: "Our purpose is to construct and market [note the word] an automobile designed for everyday wear and tear—business, professional, and family use." The car would be simple, convenient, compact, and cheap.

The Model T was everything Henry Ford promised. It was sturdy, it was dependable, and it was cheap. The price came down and down. It reached bottom with the Ford runabout, which was sold at just $250. In 1915, Ford advertised in 143 newspapers in fifty-one cities that if the company could make and sell 300,000 cars that year, every purchaser would get a rebate of from forty to sixty dollars. People bought and urged their friends to buy. Ford made the cars, sold them, and paid off as promised.

Pioneering with assembly-line production, Henry Ford put a large part of the population of the United States on wheels. Innumerable jokes about his tin lizzie were told and retold. Ford collected and treasured all of them he could get. He said they were his best advertising—and free advertising. The Ford Motor Company made and sold fifteen million Model T's before production was stopped in 1927 to make way for the almost equally famous Model A.

Henry Ford was an ingenious mechanic, an inspired production man. He was a square dancer, an ice skater, and the camping companion of Thomas Edison, Harvey Firestone, and the naturalist John Burroughs. He was an antiquarian who restored whole villages, yet said that all history was bunk. In 1914, when the Ford Motor Company was making $20 million a year, he instituted a minimum wage scale of five dollars for an eight-hour working day, high wages then, and he got all the publicity out of the move that he could. In December, 1915, he and a strange crew of zealots and idealists sailed to Europe on a Ford Peace Ship to bring an end to World War One. Henry Ford was many things, but he was insistently and consistently a marketer.

Ford made an automotive product for the mass market, packaged it for mass sale, advertised in the mass media. He used every means he or his associates could devise to attract attention to his cars themselves or to his cars through him. He never stopped telling people what he had to sell and why they should buy it. As a marketer Henry Ford used to the utmost, and effectively, one of the strongest of all marketing forces—advertising.

Whether or not he knows it, every American motorist drives a foreign car or one that has been barely naturalized. The materials of which it is made have come from North and South America, Europe, Africa, Asia, and Australia. The single most important item in the American economy, the automobile may be as American as Detroit, but it is as foreign as India, Japan, Morocco, Borneo, Sumatra, Nigeria, Argentina, and a score of other countries which provide the raw materials for its parts.

The car is a primary example of materials and components brought together from widespread markets before production can begin and the marketing of the finished article get under way. Iron, zinc, rubber, wheat straw, antimony, jute, hides, lead, lumber, paper, nickel, paint, plastics, and other materials all go into it. Without the marketing and marshaling of materials from around the world, the automobile could not be manufactured in Detroit or anywhere else in the United States.

The automobile is also an example of the survival of bargaining in a major consumer purchase. Car buying and selling is a direct descendant of horse trading and is carried on in much the same way. The buyer does not examine a car's teeth, but he does try—and seldom succeeds—to outwit the dealer or the salesman when he comes to "trade" his sizzling new car of a year or two ago, which does not seem such a sizzler anymore, for a new one with a shinier coat that he thinks will really gallop.

There is really no set price on a new automobile. The price can be moved up or down by flexible trade-in allowances and the number and cost of accessories such as hub caps, rear-view mirrors, more ornate steering wheels, metal or vinyl tops, and all the rest. The markups on all of these gadgets and decorations are very high. The public has been taught to expect to trade every few years, and the automotive industry does all it can to encourage people in the expectation. By the time a new model is released for sale with all the breathless wonder that can be made to surround its advent, it has already been outmoded by newer models in the planning or design stages, perhaps already in existence as test vehicles.

The automobile is the prime example in marketing of direct

factory to retail-outlet distribution. Though parts, accessories, and used cars are wholesaled, most new automobiles of standard makes go to retailers with no intervention by wholesalers. General Motors, Chrysler, and Ford, the so-called Big Three, all operate in this manner. Dealers operate under franchises, or licensing agreements, with the manufacturers. They have exclusive rights to market cars of given makes or particular brands of those makes in their territories, but under manufacturer restrictions.

Automobile manufacturers exert strong control over their dealers. Under the terms of his franchise the manufacturer can dictate the minimum amount of capital the dealer must invest, what floor space he must have for display, what facilities for maintenance and repair, even what management the dealer must have and the size of his sales force. The manufacturer expects the dealer to sell his quota of new cars, and the dealer expects the manufacturer to supply the cars he can sell.

In the 1930's, dealers, organized as an association, complained bitterly of coercive methods used by the manufacturers, particularly that they were forced to overstock on cars and to develop unnecessarily large and expensive facilities. Investigation by the Federal Trade Commission followed, and a huge report was given Congress in 1939. To the disappointment of the dealers, the report found most of their charges unjustified and that not the manufacturers but often dealers were guilty of price-fixing on both new and used cars and of other practices working to deny the consumer the benefits of competitive selling.

Automobile dealers pay the manufacturers an advertising allowance on each new car, and generally they are glad to pay it. It is this advertising in magazines and newspapers, on radio and television, which keeps the car-buying public informed, sells them on the beauty and performance of each year's new models, and whets their desire to drive and be seen in the latest and flashiest automobiles.

There have been more than three thousand makes of cars

made and sold in the United States. Now only four manufacturers, each with many models in a line of cars under a string of brand names, remain. Many good automobiles, some of them famous, have disappeared. Studebaker and Packard went not long ago. Hupmobile, Reo, Pierce-Arrow, Kissel Kar, Lozier, Franklin, Hudson, Chalmers, Chandler, Overland, Stutz were sound and popular cars. The once very popular Oakland became the Pontiac, just as the Maxwell became the first Chrysler. Some makes vanished in company mergers. Others went out of existence when their makers died and their heirs wished to liquidate. Some makes suffered fatally from poor engineering or poor management or other of the ills and circumstances to which any business is liable.

Many of the thousands of makes of American automobiles are no more because they were not skillfully marketed. Perhaps they were overpriced. Perhaps they did not fit the needs of motorists. Perhaps they were badly designed. Often they were inadequately or clumsily advertised.

— 7 —

Advertising as Marketing

Salesmen market necessities and luxuries; articles you know and many you have never heard of. There are salesmen everywhere. The Bureau of the Census counts more than 4.5 million of them. Some are salesmen for wholesale houses and cover large territories calling on retail customers and prospects. Others remain behind the counters of department stores, bakeries, and hobby shops. One man may be selling thousands of tons of cement for the construction of part of an interstate highway while another man or woman sells a ballpoint pen. The barker shouting hoarsely outside a carnival sideshow is a salesman; so is the highly trained engineer marketing ponderous and intricate machinery or computer memory circuits.

Many people still think of salesmen as door-to-door canvassers with a memorized spiel and a hypnotic voice who, before you know what has happened, talk you into buying a vacuum cleaner, a set of encyclopedias, or a hundred dollars' worth of magazines for "just the cost of the postage." Salesmen and saleswomen of this kind still exist, but the modern salesman is more apt to be well educated and thoroughly informed about the product he sells, the market, and the qualities of competitive products. Because of the unpleasant connotation of "salesmen" in some quarters, reputable salesmen of reputable products are often called by other titles. In some lines the salesman is a "sales engineer." The salesmen of pharmaceutical houses who call on physicians are known as "detail men." In an advertising agency the salesman may be an "account executive." In order to impress customers and prospects, many top salesmen carry the title of "vice-president." Many companies call their salesmen "representatives." They are.

They are also marketers, and they work hard at marketing. Salesmen may work on salary or commission or both, and generally they are well paid. The skills of productive salesmen are at a premium; and it is a truism in business that those who bring the money in take more of it out than those who merely produce the product.

Just like the members of industrial unions, doctors, schoolteachers, librarians, hardware merchants, and all the others, salesmen congregate in huge and noisy conventions. In sales meetings, company executives inform them of new products or product changes, of newly set sales quotas, of what percentage increase is expected of them, and generally try to whip them into a fury of competitive sales activity. Get out there and sell! Get the order!

Salesmen do just that, but their selling is personal. A salesman can call on only one prospect at a time. Mass selling of mass-produced products calls for another kind of salesmanship— advertising.

Advertising is as old as trade. It goes back to the street cries of peddlers. Street criers shouted the sales of slaves and cattle in ancient Greece. Advertising messages in Latin were chanted on the streets of Rome. William Shakespeare made a song of the street cries of peddlers in *The Winter's Tale.*

> ". . . Come buy of me; come buy, come buy;
> Buy, lads, or else your lasses cry."

Advertising broke into print almost as soon as Johann Gutenberg developed printing from movable type in fifteenth-century Germany English newspapers of the sixteenth century carried advertising, and advertising appeared on cards and handbills as well. By the eighteenth century, advertising was so prevalent in newspapers and in the first magazines that both Joseph Addison and Dr. Samuel Johnson wrote about it; Johnson saying that the claims of advertisers for soap, bed coverings, and lotions were so numerous and so exaggerated that advertising had almost achieved perfection.

The newspapers of colonial America had columns of advertising for rum, hardware, runaway slaves, indentured servants, the return of lost or stolen property, wagons, entertainments, and even for dancing schools. Benjamin Franklin, Paul Revere, and George Washington all advertised.

Throughout the nineteenth century in the United States, patent-medicine advertising flourished on billboards, sandwich men, placards, in the newspapers, and in the most respected magazines. Almost every one of these nostrums was guaranteed to cure everything from a broken neck to freckles, and the claims of many of the advertisers put to shame the medicine shows that hypnotized audiences in pioneer towns. Advertising of more substantial kinds for worthwhile products could scarcely compete.

The great surge of advertising came in the last quarter of the nineteenth century with the advent of mass magazines of large circulation. The advertiser could use these to sell his wares across the country. By the 1890's, periodicals carried as many pages of advertising as of editorial matter. Thread, silverware, jewelry, cosmetics, clothes, shoes, foods, watches, lard, carriages, and then automobiles. The advertising looks old-fashioned now, but that is mostly because of the print and illustrations. The claims are much the same.

Advertising was in full swing in the United States in the early years of the twentieth century. Ever since, it has swung higher and higher. Whereas it was all in print at first, it reverted to speech with radio, and blossomed into animated picture as well as sound with television. Today advertising is almost inescapable in the United States. We are surrounded and almost engulfed by it. Newspapers, radio, television, billboards, signs, handbills, samples, a half-dozen commercials or more in every half hour of television programs are the most noticeable. In the United States, marketers spend about $17 billion a year on advertising.

Advertising has just one purpose, to sell. It is persuasion, sometimes gentle, sometimes harsh. It is intended to arouse desires which lead to purchase. Come buy my wares! is the insistently repeated cry. Whatever the guise in which it appears—humor, stern adjuration, formal announcement, vaudevillelike comedy, singing commercial, or stark want ad—that is the plea. You may find the advertising nauseating, interesting, ridiculous, pleasing, or abominable. It does not much matter. The idea is to make you so familiar with a brand name, whether it is that of a car, a cereal, or a detergent, that when you come to buy you will remember that name and buy that brand. It works. When confronted by an unbranded, unadvertised article, the consumer is so indoctrinated he is apt to suspect it is inferior. Else why does not the maker affix his name or trademark, and why is it not advertised?

The advertising of manufacturers is not directed only at consumers. It is meant to attract dealers to handle a line because buyers have been presold before they enter a store. Here, marketing jumps all the way from maker to user, but the result comes in the retail outlet. Most national advertising in print or electronic media does not carry prices. These are set at the retail level. It is the local advertising in newspapers which tells how much a product costs, where it can be bought, and when it is on sale at bargain prices. Local radio and television are also used for this purpose.

Advertising differs for established products and for new or changed products. A brand of a long-familiar staple, say, baking powder or a well-known make of car, is often reminder advertising. Advertising for a new product has to sell both a new idea and sometimes one that is frighteningly strange as well as the product—frozen food, air travel, oil heat all had to be introduced by long-continued educational advertising.

People feared that oil heat might set fire to their homes or blow them up, and coal dealers did all they could to make them think so. The idea of electricity and a chemical refrigerant could terrify. The icebox with pure frozen water chopped in winter from some lake and delivered daily by the iceman was what householders knew. Advertising had to market safety, reliability, and convenience as well as "Frigidaire." Advertising made that one pioneer brand so well known that its name almost became generic.

Women were used to silk stockings. The idea that stockings of synthetic material could be as comfortable, as wearable, and as flattering had to be sold through testing, sampling, and strong advertising before Nylons could drive silk stockings from the popular market.

People knew and trusted canned foods. When they were introduced in 1929, quick-frozen foods had to be explained and defended. The producer placed consignments with twenty participating stores in one city chosen as a test market. It took large newspaper space to announce and describe discovery of the quick-frozen process and explain how to thaw and prepare the foods. A motion picture describing Clarence Birdseye's discovery and development of the process and the advantages of quick-frozen foods was shown in five theaters and before clubs and other organizations. A traveling electric sign telling the story was moved from store to store. Newspaper advertising for the frozen meats, fruits, and vegetables was continuous. One advertisement after another featured quick-frozen sole, haddock, oysters, spring lamb, spinach, and other foods.

Advertising had to break down resistance to something strange and suspicious, awaken interest and curiosity, get people to experiment. When this initial marketing caught on, quick-frozen foods were placed on sale in other cities and then nationally. They were accepted. A huge new industry, complete from farm and ranch down through processing plants, wholesalers, and retailers, was built. Quick-frozen foods were established as part of the American diet.

The marketing of a "new and improved" product calls for educational advertising of a different kind. Already accustomed to the brand which may have been on the market for years, customers must be convinced that the changes are for the better. The manufacturer is out to maintain and if possible to enlarge what is generally called his "share of the market" in competition with that of other producers of like products. He has to be careful. The "new and improved" product has to be marketed without damaging the reputation expensively created for the old and unimproved product.

Every year the advertising for each make of new car stresses its great beauty, speed, economy, and infinite desirability. One inevitable result is to make the car buyer wonder what is the matter with the car he bought last year, which was also described as more beautiful, more economical, and infinitely more desirable. Cars do improve. Once you had to crank them. Came the self-starter, four-wheel brakes, coil springs, torsion bars, and other actual improvements. There is some reason—though scarcely enough—why the same make of car sells for four or five times as much in 1970, as it did twenty or twenty-five years ago.

Coffee has been advertised—first for medicinal purposes— for at least three centuries. At the start of this century it was usually unbranded, bought loose, "fresh roasted" by the pound. The purchaser took his coffee beans home and ground them in his own coffee mill, which was attached to the kitchen wall in most homes, or he had the grocer grind it for him when he bought it. There was a pleasant smell in many old-fashioned grocery stores. Then came the packaging of already ground coffee and its sale under various brand names. Advertisers celebrated the merits of their brands and implied the demerits of the others. Containers were improved. Cans were hermetically sealed. Branded coffees were especially ground for use in the ordinary coffeepot, in electric percolators, or in drip contraptions.

Then came instant coffee in powdered form. All the housewife had to do was slip a spoonful into a cup and pour hot water over it. Every brand of instant coffee was as wonderful as the advertising copywriter could make it. Recently, freeze-dried coffee has come on the market. It, of course, is the ultimate. Every brand of it is richer, darker, more aromatic, and more satisfying than every other brand. The freeze-drying process is hailed in advertisements as the discovery of the century and its results as the biggest boon to mankind since the invention of the wheel.

The trouble is that most of the processors of freeze-dried coffee also make and sell regular ground coffee and powdered instant coffee. They cannot say or intimate that these too are not marvelous. They must advertise in such a way that consumers rush out to buy freeze-dried coffee in addition to, not instead of, the coffee they market in other forms. They must avoid making the coffee drinker wonder why he did not die of malnutrition or waste away of dissatisfaction before any new and improved product was introduced.

There are several well-established theories of advertising. One is that a product must be advertised continuously and frequently. Repetition adds to the effect created by earlier advertising. The advertising must be continuous because young consumers are always coming into the market and older ones leaving it. As is always said (Charles Coolidge Parlin said it first about 1912), "A market is not a standing army but a parade." Another advertising theory is that a durable product of high price must be advertised regularly so that consumers will be informed and have a favorable impression of it when they are ready to buy.

The corollary is that inexpensive and frequently purchased items must be continually advertised to presell customers and establish brand loyalty. Else they may be tempted to buy competitive products.

Another theory—really more a rule of thumb than a theory—is that you had better advertise because surely your competitors will. The proverbial bit of advertising wisdom is that "advertising pays." This is fact even if sometimes hard to prove for a given product. What is sure is that if you do not advertise you cannot market in quantity; and that if you cease advertising, lack of sales will soon put you out of business. Once-popular products have disappeared from the market when advertising for them was discontinued because the producer had the mistaken belief that his product had been established for all time. As the nineteenth-century English poet and historian Thomas Babington, Lord Macaulay said, "Nothing except the mint can make money without advertising."

Products which cost little to make and comparatively little to ship are the most insistently marketed through advertising. With these, advertising is more expensive than production. Cosmetics, toiletries, razor blades, aspirin and aspirin compounds, even when, as with many washing-machine compounds, they are products of the same manufacturer. The idea is to sell them all.

One headache, supposed to be particularly severe, can be alleviated only by a brand name which was dreamed up by an advertising agency before a drug company manufactured a product to attach to it. One brand of aspirin is pure aspirin, the suggestion being made that other brands are not, though by definition aspirin, a derivative of salicylic acid, is aspirin. Branded razor blades, so improved every week or two that they seem in danger of being improved to extinction, advertise by figuratively cutting each other's throats. The toothpastes promise all kinds of benefits, and the deodorants and breath sweeteners almost resort to blackmail. If you don't use specified brands, no one will like you.

There are reputable kinds of quieter advertising which contrast markedly with the feverishly competitive. Institutional advertising is used by organizations to underline the integrity and responsibility of an industry or a corporation. Trade association advertising is not for brands but for products made and marketed by all the members of the association. It is "Eat More Meat" for the packing industry before their owners advertise their particular brands of sausage, bacon, bologna, ham, and other meats. Oranges, apples, walnuts are all association-advertised in this way.

Large corporations whose basic sales are to the manufacturing industry use institutional advertising to establish their identity in the public mind. Sometimes this advertising is also used to build internal employee morale. The Union Carbide Corporation was formed in 1917 by a merger of five companies. It makes and distributes a few consumer items—an insect repellant, an antifreeze, flashlight batteries, and a plastic food wrap—but most of its more than sixteen thousand different products go to industry. With about 120,000 employees around the world, the company is so large that many working in its various subsidiaries and subdivisions had little awareness of the corporation as a whole, and the general public knew Union Carbide only as a name. For both these reasons, it entered into an elaborate television schedule and some print advertising to make itself known as "The Discovery Company."

Without advertising, successful mass marketing is, if not impossible, very unlikely. It is all too easy to criticize advertising adversely. Some of it earns all the disparagement it gets. Other advertising deserves the admiration it arouses both for its intrinsic excellence and for the part it plays in getting products and services to those who need them.

The consumer benefits from sound and honest advertising. It tells him what has been produced in competition for his favor and purchase. It gives him a description or specifications of what he can expect. It tells him where to get what he seeks. The advertising for a branded product gives him some guarantee of its worth. The maker has put his name on it. He is responsible for it. Usually the branded and advertised product is a better article at a lower price. Mass advertising as a part of mass marketing makes the manufacturing economies of mass production possible.

– 8 –

Mass Marketing: Coca-Cola

Coca-Cola has to be the most successfully mass-marketed product in the world.

In 1886, when there were just eight soda fountains in the entire state of Georgia, Dr. John S. Pemberton, an Atlanta druggist, mixed the first Coca-Cola syrup in an iron pot in the backyard of his home. He made and sold twenty-five gallons of it that year, sold it for $50, and spent $46 of it for advertising. The first Coca-Cola advertisement was an oilcloth streamer to attach to drugstore awnings. It read simply: "Coca-Cola—Delicious and Refreshing."

After Pemberton's death in 1886, another Atlanta wholesale and retail druggist, Asa G. Candler, became sole owner of the Coca-Cola formula. Candler dropped his other business interest to devote all of his time to the manufacture and marketing of the beverage. He organized The Coca-Cola Company as a Georgia corporation with a capital stock of $100,000 in 1892 and that same year budgeted $11,401.78 for advertising. The trade name Coca-Cola was registered with the United States Patent Office on January 31, 1893. Expansion was rapid.

The first Coca-Cola syrup manufacturing plant outside Atlanta was opened in Dallas, Texas. The first Coca-Cola bottling was begun in Vicksburg, Mississippi. Coca-Cola was advertised everywhere on calendars, serving trays, soda-fountain urns, clocks, and painted walls. By 1895, Asa Candler could say, "Coca-Cola is now sold and drunk in every state and territory in the United States."

The Coca-Cola Company erected the first new building of its own in Atlanta in 1898. The next year it granted large-scale bottling rights to a company in Chattanooga, Tennessee. In 1900, Coca-Cola instituted its fundamental policy of granting exclusive bottling rights in territories across the country to independent businessmen who then operated, under contract, locally owned Coca-Cola bottling and distributing plants.

By 1901 the annual advertising budget of Coca-Cola was $100,000. Ten years later, with more branch syrup-manufacturing plants around the country and more Coca-Cola bottlers, the figure reached $1 million. Coca-Cola was advertised in nationally circulated mass magazines now as well as in the familiar *Coca-Cola* in Spencerian script, red against white or white against red, on signs and displays. In 1915, Coca-Cola adopted one of its most successful forms of advertising, its distinctively shaped bottle. Like its trade name, the Coca-Cola bottle is patented.

In 1919, Asa Candler and his associates sold Coca-Cola for $25 million to new and even more energetic Atlanta interests headed by Ernest Woodruff. The Coca-Cola Company was reincorporated in Delaware and stock was placed on sale to the public at $40 per share. Today, exclusive of accumulated dividends, that one share is worth about $7,000.

It was under Robert W. Woodruff, who succeeded his father as president in 1922, remained in office until 1946, and was on the company board until 1955, that the business was revolutionized. Robert Woodruff introduced a host of new marketing methods. The six-bottle family carton was developed for the carry-home market. Refrigerated coolers were installed in a wide network of outlets. In offices and factories men and women could purchase Coca-Cola cold from cabinets and then from automatic vending machines. Automatic fountain dispensers facilitated proper mixing of syrup and carbonated water at soda fountains.

Points of sale for Coca-Cola were multiplied in the huge and ever-growing domestic market, and new markets were sought overseas. The company, which had begun to sell abroad as early as 1915, pushed its foreign business actively in the 1920's. After the United States entered World War Two in 1941, Robert Woodruff issued an order: "See that every man in uniform gets a bottle of Coca-Cola for five cents wherever he is and whatever it costs."

This was patriotic altruism. It was also, despite any loss to the company at that time, good business. During World War Two, more than five billion bottles of Coke went to service men and women, in addition to that served in dispensers in battle areas. Sixty-four complete Coca-Cola bottling plants were shipped abroad and set up near combat areas. To service people, Coke was home. They liked it. They continued to like it, and the market for Coca-Cola grew again. Today the sales and profits of The Coca-Cola Company are about one half in and one half outside of the United States.

Early, Coca-Cola was almost too successful. Its success attracted ambitious imitators who made and marketed competitive beverages. Coca-Cola was forced to protect its identity in numerous lawsuits. The drink became known familiarly as "Coke." There was danger that this might become a general name under which anyone could make and sell a beverage of like appearance when a customer asked for "Coke."

Coca-Cola fought its case all the way to the Supreme Court, which decided that the name "Coke" was the sole property of The Coca-Cola Company. In delivering the court's opinion, Chief Justice Oliver Wendell Holmes said, ". . . It means a single thing coming from a single source, and well known to the community." The trade name Coke was also patented and is used on labels and in some Coca-Cola advertising.

Coca-Cola is an immense worldwide enterprise. Coca-Cola syrup is manufactured in eleven plants in different parts of the United States. There are nine hundred independent Coca-Cola bottling companies in this country. With other bottling plants abroad, Coke is now sold in 137 countries. Coke is known from the Arctics to the tropics. It is estimated that 90 percent of the world's population can recognize the distinctive Coca-Cola bottle. The popularity of Coke in the United States is matched in the rest of North America and on the other continents. Foreigners visiting the United States are often surprised to see the signs which tell them that Coke is the same word in many languages and that Coca-Cola is known in this country as well as in theirs. One figure issued by the company beggars the imagination. Every day more than 100 million drinks of Coke are sold and drunk around the world.

In the United States, people get thirsty. So do people in other countries. They drink Coca-Cola, often several times a day.

Two people—or three or four—meet on the street. "Let's go get a Coke." They seek out the nearest soda fountain and drink as they chat.

Unexpected guests drop in. "Care for a Coke?" They always do. If the guests are expected, the Coca-Cola is ready, and the ice.

Drinking Coca-Cola is a pleasant habit. It is a social pleasure. It is a gracious gesture on the part of the host and welcome refreshment to the entertained.

"Ma! We're out of Coke!" Someone hurries to the store.

The basic reasons for worldwide acceptance and consumption of this kind are simple. As it has to be with any commonly purchased and used item, the first and most basic reason is the product. Coca-Cola is made today on the same formula that Dr. Pemberton used when he mixed his first batch of the syrup. The ingredients are a compound of essential oils and flavors, highly refined sugar, pure caramel for color, and, whether bottled or mixed at the fountain, carbonated water.

Many people have asked what the exact ingredients and proportions are. That, of course, is a carefully guarded secret of The Coca-Cola Company. The formula is kept in the vaults of two banks, and these can be opened only by action of the company's board of directors. The formula has been divulged only once. In answer to the question asked once more, this time in Detroit in 1967, Coca-Cola's president said, "I'll give you the precise formula. You can get out your pencils and write it down. Coca-Cola is like a little girl: sugar 'n spice and everything nice." The company likes to quote the Kansas sage and journalist William Allen White who wrote, "Coca-Cola is . . . a decent thing, honestly made, universally distributed . . ."

The next most important reason for the marketing success of Coca-Cola is that people like it. Obviously all kinds of people all over the world do not buy and drink a beverage which they do not like. Why they like it, who can say? The taste? The lift? The coolness? The feel of the cold glass or bottle in the hand? The companionship of those who stop by for a Coke? A combination of these and other reactions is likely, but there is no answer. One likes or dislikes, and it is futile to try to find out why. *De gustibus non est disputandum* (there is no disputing concerning tastes) is a saying which has lasted a long time because it is true.

The third basic reason for the success in mass marketing Coca-Cola is its advertising.

That advertising has never changed. It is in essence the same that it was in 1886 when Dr. Pemberton described it as delicious and refreshing. Though the wording has changed slightly in the eighty-five years since it was first introduced, Coca-Cola has never claimed to be anything else. "The pause that refreshes . . . Things go better with Coke . . . Drink Coca-Cola —The real thing . . . Coke has the taste you never get tired of . . ."

Coca-Cola was spending $20 million a year in 1948 to say just about what Dr. Pemberton said. It spent $30 million in 1953, and in 1959 its annual advertising budget went to $40 million. It spends even larger sums now. Does this advertising pay? In 1928 The Coca-Cola Company manufactured and marketed its six billionth gallon of Coca-Cola syrup. Net sales of The Coca-Cola Company and its subsidiaries in 1969 were $1,365,443,068 and net profit after taxes was $121,019,702.

Coca-Cola advertising is directed to everybody everywhere because everybody is a potential customer for Coke. In drugstores, in food markets, in coolers and automatic dispensers, in motels, filling stations, on trucks, on clocks are the red-and-white Coca-Cola signs. It is hard to escape them. They are a constant reminder that Coca-Cola is where you are. The Coca-Cola name is a familiar part of the scene whether you are on Broadway, in Piccadilly Circus, in an Arkansas motel, or in a sandwich shop on Cape Cod. Coke is within reach at the fountain, in the filling station, and from the shop or office machine.

In its more elaborate print or television advertising, Coca-Cola is shown in the company of pleasant-looking people. For many years it was shown with an attractive girl seated alone at a drugstore counter. The girl was pretty and dressed all in white. The conviction is established that Coca-Cola is socially acceptable, that it is of superior taste and quality.

Coca-Cola never lets you forget its presence and its desirability. The company's advertising is unremitting, and its appeal is consistent. It is a carefully planned part of its entire marketing effort. Coca-Cola is not a necessity but a pleasure, and it is marketed for its pleasurable qualities. The housewife may notice that the supply in the family refrigerator is dwindling and make a note on her shopping list to replenish it, but most Coca-Cola is purchased on impulse. You are hot and thirsty or tired. You see the familiar sign. Impulse buying of this kind must be stimulated by reminder advertising. It reminds you that you like the product, that it is there, and you buy. One of the most effective places for advertising of this kind is where the product is obtainable. Thus Coca-Cola makes extensive use of point-of-sale reminders in the drugstore, the market, wherever you can see the name and find Coke.

In some of its advertising, Coca-Cola uses a variety of appeal to avoid monotony, to present the glass or bottle in different settings and situations, but its primary appeal has always remained with its script trade name, its red-and-white colors, and the shape of the Coca-Cola bottle. It uses slogans to capitalize on familiarity and gain the other values of repetition. "The pause that refreshes" was introduced as long ago as 1929. The value of any slogan lies in its durability, its use year after year until you cannot see or hear it without thinking of the product to which it refers.

"Enjoy Coca-Cola" is the current slogan. It is on store-signs, on automatic vending machines, on the sides of Coca-Cola bottlers' trucks, on cartons of bottles, on the white helmets, and sewn on the back and front of the uniforms of Coca-Cola services workers. In 1970 something new was added to the long unchanged Coca-Cola brand name or logo mark. A curving flash of white underlines the name wherever it appears. This is intended to enhance visibility, attract more attention, and strengthen product identity.

Product quality, public acceptance, and broadly directed, widespread, ubiquitous advertising are joined in the international mass marketing of Coca-Cola. These three elements merge into a marketing force which has established Coca-Cola around the world with almost awesome sureness.

— 9 —

Communications Marketing: Xerox

Ten years ago, comparatively few people knew the name "Xerox." Today it is generally familiar. It means a copying device, a series of such devices. More comprehensively, it means communications: graphic reproduction, texts, books, magazines, computer-data systems—and television spectaculars. It also means scientific achievement in helping to design rocket engines and even to convert sunlight into a power source. Yet the giant Xerox Corporation was not formed until 1961.

Marketing did not invent the Xerox copier. Marketing did induce the extremely rapid growth, then accelerate even this pace, which in a single decade established the Xerox product as an essential tool in education, government, and business. Marketing established Xerox in the public consciousness as a corporate entity. Until marketing took over, the Xerox copier and its inventor and developer were almost unknown.

Chester Carlson was born in Seattle, Washington, in 1906. He graduated in physics from the California Institute of Technology in 1930 and found a job in the patent department of an electronics company in New York. At night he studied law in New York University. His scientific and engineering training made him impatient of the chore of copying notes from books and documents while pursuing his legal studies in the public libraries. He began the study of electrostatics and photoconductors in search of an easier way. In 1937 he filed his first patent application for a process he dubbed "electrophotography."

A year later Carlson had constructed a dry electrostatic copying device which worked when he tried it in a laboratory in Astoria, Long Island, on October 22, 1938. He looked for financial backers to start manufacturing. He could find none, but in 1944, by which time he owned a patent on his "electrophotographic apparatus," he managed to get it demonstrated at the Battelle Memorial Institute in Columbus, Ohio. Impressed by its performance, Battelle, an industrial research organization, agreed to carry out initial development work for somewhat more than a half share of any profits which might ensue.

In Rochester, New York, Dr. John H. Dessauer, research director of Haloid, a small manufacturer of photographic and photocopy papers, read an account of Carlson's device in a scientific journal. Haloid, which was not prospering, was seeking a new line. Under its president, Joseph C. Wilson, it obtained sole rights to develop the Carlson process commercially. Haloid worked intensively to raise funds, improve the process, and get into production. It gave the process a name, "xerography" from the Greek *xeros,* meaning dry, and *graphein,* to write.

Haloid marketed the first Xerox Model A Copier, a flat-plate device, in 1950. The company built a special and very aggressive sales force, and the Model A sold. More investment capital was obtained, and Haloid developed a new model, the Copyflo. This was the first Xerox copier that could make copies automatically on ordinary paper either from documents or from microfilm images of them.

Notoriously, government lives on paper. It makes copies in duplicate, triplicate, or quintuplicate of every paper it can lay its hands on. Business must continually make copies of contracts, correspondence, and innumerable forms. Schools often need multiple copies of material under study. There is hardly an operational organization of any size that does not need to make copies of written material it handles. To all of these—once they knew about it—an automatic copier that could reproduce on ordinary paper was a boon.

New Xerox models were produced, and Haloid set out to market them to the full. It imported two men in their thirties from Philadelphia where they had worked for a coal company and with them proceeded to build a large and unusually effective marketing organization. As a result, Haloid sales, which had been only $7 million in 1947, rose to $21 million in 1955 and $25 million in 1957. As the Xerox process was now the company's most important property, the company name was changed to Haloid Xerox, Inc., in 1957.

In March, 1960, Xerox introduced its 914 copier, so called because it can make copies on paper up to nine by fourteen inches in size. This was the first fully automatic dry copier in the office-equipment industry, and with it Xerox struck out for larger sales in the world market and unbridled expansion in many forms of communications.

The Xerox copier is not a mass product to be mass marketed to everybody. It is an expensive and sensitive device which needs exposure and demonstration to a select market. Advertising alone cannot accomplish this. A large force of salesmen had to be recruited and trained. With sales booming, the Xerox sales force numbered about a thousand in 1962. Plans were made to treble that number. In 1962, Xerox had thirty-two branch sales offices. It decided to establish seventy-five within four years.

Physically the 914 Xerox copier is a substantial product. It weighs nearly 650 pounds. A salesman cannot carry many around in his sample case. This meant that Xerox had to open demonstration centers and to exhibit its copier and its prowess at conventions and professional meetings—to show it wherever potential government and corporation customers gathered.

How successful this marketing procedure was can be gauged

by an impressive list of early purchasers: the White House, the Senate, the House, Buckingham Palace, Parliament, du Pont, Ford, General Electric, General Motors, Westinghouse, Boeing, Douglas, General Dynamics, most of the large insurance companies, and the labor unions. In 1951 Haloid had negotiated a partnership with the Rank Organization of Great Britain to create Rank Xerox, Ltd., with offices in London. By 1962, Rank Xerox (which the Xerox Corporation now controls through majority stock ownership) was marketing Xerox copiers in many countries through subsidiaries in Germany, France, Australia, Mexico, Italy, and Japan. Xerox made no secret of the fact that, despite strong competition from perhaps forty manufacturers of copying devices, it was out to become a world leader in graphic communications.

Xerox currently has many more than the three thousand salesmen it planned for 1967, and it did not acquire them by happenstance. It recruits vigorously for marketing personnel and knows the kind of salesmen it is looking for. It seeks men with personality, high IQ's, good judgment, and the ability to deal with people. Earnings—partly salary, partly commission—can be high, but the salesman must earn them. Recent college graduates hired for its sales force undergo months of intensive training. Experienced salesmen hired are also schooled in Xerox products and Xerox marketing methods. Both new and older salesmen return for sales refresher courses. A salesman can advance to head an account team—a marketing team—and then, if he proves his worth to the company, become a branch sales office manager. In 1965 a top Xerox executive foresaw the day when the corporation's annual revenue would hit $1 billion and would need twelve thousand people for its marketing. He underestimated. Total operating revenue of the Xerox Corporation was nearer $1.5 billion in 1969.

Besides its large and growing force of aggressive salesmen, its demonstrations and exhibitions, Xerox needed the other primary marketing force, advertising. Determined on rapid growth and expansion, it went into intensive advertising directed to definite goals. In 1961 the corporation's total marketing expenditures were $14 million; in 1967 they were $23.7 million. During this same period its annual advertising investment went from $990,000 to $14 million.

Xerox advertising is planned not only to reach buyers, but also to create an image of Xerox as a dynamic and expanding corporation. Its advertising is intended to make Xerox favorably known to the leaders in government and industry; to create a corporation image which distinguishes it from its competitors and wins public approval; and to provide visual demonstrations of its copiers, particularly the 914. Xerox used marketing research to find out what kind of advertising in what media would best serve these ends. Then, though it did not eschew print advertising, it decided to concentrate on documentary, public-service advertising on television.

Television is a mass advertising medium. It is *the* mass advertising medium, seen and heard by all kinds of people, young and old. Many viewers could not possibly be customers for Xerox equipment, but research showed that programs of the kind the corporation selected drew a high percentage of well-educated, high-income viewers—the kind of people who influence the buying of Xerox equipment when their companies or government departments are making purchase decisions.

Xerox began its television advertising in November, 1961, with sponsorship of *CBS Reports*. Since that time it has sponsored many major television programs. As the Xerox Corporation invaded related fields—book publishing, education, data systems—it advanced from pure documentaries into other kinds of informational programs and even into the arts. It has sponsored *The Making of the President, The Kremlin, Let My People Go, Ballet for Skeptics, The Glass Menagerie, A Midsummer Night's Dream,* and other quality programs. The basic idea of this advertising in which commercials are kept to a minimum is to identify Xerox with excellence.

Xerox also strives to identify itself with social causes. In 1968 it ran *Of Black America,* eight prime-time programs, without commercials, showing black contributions to American history. The British Broadcasting Company created and successfully presented in 1969 a series of television films showing the ideas and events of Western civilization over the past sixteen hundred years. Xerox granted $300,000 to National Education Television, and the first of the thirteen one-hour-long shows titled *Civilization* was shown over 185 educational television stations in October, 1970. It is planned to rerun the series in the fall of 1971.

Xerox itself is a contemporary marketing phenomenon. It has spent many millions of dollars in research and development, $83.7 million in 1969 alone. From its rather crude Model A copier through its standard 914 it has advanced to the manufacture and marketing of highly sophisticated copiers and systems. One is its 3600-III, which reproduces halftone illustrations at the rate of sixty a minute. Another is the Xerox Telecopier. By telephone it transmits copies of drawings, photographs, orders, or other documents anywhere in the country in six minutes or less. In 1969, a Xerox subsystem went to Mars aboard the Mariner 6 and 7 spacecraft. That same year a Xerox copier was installed in the Presidential jet. Xerox equipment is in use in about 200,000 organizations, large and small, in the United States and Canada. Rank Xerox now markets in sixty-nine countries.

Xerox products are marketed to a selective, able-to-buy and able-to-use market primarily composed of government (the largest purchaser), corporations, and institutions. In its total effort the Xerox Corporation exemplifies large-scale attack on a sprawling market composed of communications in many forms. Xerox owns and operates the Boston textbook firm of Ginn and Company. It is in periodical publishing with its American

Education Publications which, among other juvenile magazines, issues *My Weekly Reader* in seven editions, one each for kindergarten through sixth grade. This wholly-owned subsidiary also conducts children's book clubs and a record club.

Xerox has published books under other imprints. Perhaps the happiest venture here was *Alice's Adventures Under Ground,* a facsimile of the Lewis Carroll manuscript of *Alice in Wonderland* which is in the British Museum. The book was published by another Xerox subsidiary, University Microfilms, and very successfully marketed.

Around the world, the Xerox Corporation employs some 55,000 people. Its total operating revenue in 1969 was $1,482,-895,000. In the short space of one decade and in a climate generally unfavorable to new business ventures, Xerox has achieved repute and established its dominance in automatic dry electrophotostatic copying. Chester Carlson invented a device of value; Haloid, then Xerox improved it. Marketing must account for most of the rest of the corporate accomplishment.

Xerox was market oriented from the beginning. Its direction comes out of marketing, and its aims, of course, are marketing aims. As currently in many other companies, its chief executive is a marketing man. C. Peter McColough, who succeeded Joseph C. Wilson as president, is one of the two men Haloid brought in from Philadelphia in the early 1950's. The other, John W. Rutledge, is Xerox senior vice president in charge of marketing. A large, hard-selling sales force pushes Xerox copiers everywhere a prospect can be found who has a need for one of its copiers and the not inconsiderable sum needed to purchase or lease it. Publicity, promotion, and advertising parallel and support this sales activity.

Xerox is not a conservative company. Determined on rapid growth, it believes in product and marketing innovation—in taking well-considered risks, in the dynamic approach.

Its early success found it pressed for manufacturing, warehousing, laboratory, and office space. It planned a thousand-acre complex in Webster, New York, near Rochester, and it was in a hurry. Instead of shopping around for low bids, it let construction contracts on the much more expensive cost-plus basis. The corporation was convinced that at this juncture it was more important to have production facilities for what was then its new 914 than to save money.

The decision was even more daring than it appeared. Marketing analysis had shown the 914 superior to copiers made by other companies, but it had also shown that most of them were sold for about five hundred dollars, while the manufacturing cost of the 914 was about two thousand. Marketing innovation solved that. Xerox sold its 914 on a cost-per-copy basis and won.

The development of new copiers and Xerographic systems and improvements in older models keeps scientists and engineers hard at work in its plants and laboratories. Far from Rochester, Xerox has in Los Angeles what it calls a Corporate Development Group. Its assignment is to look ahead, to determine what technological advances of use to Xerox are on the way, and to decide how Xerox can use them to keep abreast or ahead of market opportunities.

Until 1969 the international offices of the Xerox Corporation were in Xerox Square in downtown Rochester. Its Business Products Group took full occupancy there, and corporate headquarters were moved to Stamford, Connecticut, within the New York metropolitan area.

Marketing built this rather formidable structure and added one more word of classical Greek derivation, the trademarked "Xerox," to the modern English vocabulary. Like the marketers of other successful products, Xerox must work to protect its name. In letters to those who use it incorrectly, and in advertising in such magazines as *The New Yorker, Business Week,* and *Fortune,* it warns against infringement. The tone is light, but the intent is serious in this advertisement.

What our trademark
lawyers have put together
let no man put asunder.

The lawyers who watch over our trademark want you to watch out how you use it.

Xerox is a registered trademark. It identifies our products. And it shouldn't be used for anything anybody else makes.

Sunder what you like, but not our trademark, please!

Sometimes marketing can be almost dangerously effective.

– 10 –

Food Marketing

Everybody does not buy a duplicating machine, but everybody eats, and we see the results of a long marketing process in food stores and taste it at our tables. Fruits and vegetables, milk, meat, and poultry, canned, packaged, or frozen foods come a long way and go through many hands before they reach the consumer. It is a continuous process, an unbroken activity. It has to be when a population of about 225 million must be fed. There can be no interruption in this marketing process. It does not take a city long to eat all the food available in its stores and warehouses, then wait hungrily for more.

Historically this was an agricultural country, with families eating the fruits and vegetables they grew and the meat animals they raised and slaughtered. That was a long time ago. Ours is largely an industrialized urban and suburban society. The number of farms decreases every year. There were 6,097,000 in 1940 but only 3,158,000, about half that number, by 1964. Now, even with Hawaii and Alaska included, the number is down to 2,895,000, with a further drop expected.

People leave the farm to work in cities. Superhighway construction bulldozes productive farms out of existence. Small farms merge into larger ones. Fortunately, the size of the average farm has increased, and improved production methods yield larger crops. Some farms are now very large, and many are no longer one-family setups but big business operations. In 1964, when the figures were reported, there were 31,401 United States farms with annual sales of $100,000 or more, and these accounted for 24 percent of all farm-product sales.

It is perhaps because we were a farm-oriented people in the past that the United States Department of Agriculture (USDA) is third in size of all the departments of the federal government, exceeded only by the Post Office and Defense. And although the number of farms and people engaged in farming steadily decreases, the Department of Agriculture continues to grow. It had 85,000 employees in 1955 but more than 105,000 in 1967—as compared with about 40,800 in the Department of Commerce and about 10,000 in the Department of Labor. It looks as if the importance paid farming by government dates from traditional interests rather than from present-day needs, but the USDA administers numerous programs. Some of them, like the national school-lunch program and providing financial crop supports, are some distance removed from actual farming, but one of the department's central concerns is farm marketing.

The USDA Consumer and Marketing Service, in cooperation with the agricultural departments of the various states, provides up-to-the-hour information on supply, demand, prices, and movements of agricultural products daily through a network of some 220 field offices. This information is printed in newspapers and trade papers and broadcast on radio and television to advise farmers, shippers, wholesalers, retailers, and everyone else concerned in the movements of foods from farm to consumer of the marketing conditions that affect them. These reports tell what crops are ready for market and whether they are in long or short supply. They tell where to sell and what the prevailing prices are; where to buy and for how much. Get up early enough in the morning and you will probably hear the farm-market reports on your local radio.

No one knows how much food is actually produced and consumed in the United States. A farmer does not make a record when he plucks and eats a tomato as he walks along the rows, nor does a boy keep count of the apples he picks and eats from a convenient tree. Suburban and even city families sometimes have their own vegetable gardens and eat the radishes, lettuce, and whatever else they grow without turning them into statistics. Overall estimates of production, though, are published by the USDA. In 1969, production of the twenty-seven principal vegetables and melons for the fresh-vegetable market came to about 221 billion hundredweight, not quite as high as in 1968, for a total farm value of $1,229,612,000.

All of this food has to get from the farm to the table. It means selling by farmers to distributors and wholesalers, trucking to wholesale markets in nearby centers, transporting by refrigerated freight car, by truck, or by air or sea to distant points, then trucking to retail outlets. All this happens before the carrots, onions, turnips, and the rest go into the shopping cart, into the family kitchen, and into the family stomachs.

At the same time, other vegetables are raised by or raised and sold to processors for canning, freezing, and sometimes for bottling. In 1969, production of the ten principal vegetable crops for commercial processing was 8,388,030 tons—and this was a big drop from the previous year.

The marketing of this food, all of it perishable when sold fresh, is complicated and, to an outsider, confusing. The produce markets of big cities are congested bedlam in the early morning hours; and those of smaller cities are the same except for size. Here, retailers buy what they think they can market to their customers—asparagus, when it is in season, from the Connecticut Valley, potatoes from Maine, Bermuda onions from Texas, cantaloupe from Delaware, and king crabs from the Aleutians. The bright green cabbage wrapped in cellophane may have come a long way before you see it on the counter in a food store. A little later in the season, it may come from a farm only a few miles distant.

A dairy farmer in Dutchess County, New York, may have about three hundred acres, perhaps half of them tillable. His herd will run from about sixty to eighty cows, mostly Holsteins, as they are big milk producers. The farm raises as much as possible of its own feed: corn, hay, sorghum grass, perhaps oats. Other feeds it must buy, and grain feeds are expensive. The farm sells its milk to a cooperative and, as it is near the state line, to the Connecticut milk shed, which pays about $1.50 more the hundredweight than the New York milk shed. If the butterfat content averages 3.4 percent in a month, there is additional remuneration. The milk is picked up by tank trucks at the farm daily or every other day; production depends upon how many of the cows are fresh at a given time and how many dried off.

If it is to be sold as fluid milk, this milk is pasteurized at the dairy, bottled or poured into cartons, and sold either for home delivery or store sales. Milk, especially from the big dairying states like Wisconsin, may reach the market in other forms—as cheese, butter, or dried, evaporated, or condensed milk. That, of course, means processing, packing, shipping, advertising, and additional marketing operations. Fluid-grade milk commands a significantly higher price than manufacturing grade. For fresh fluid milk, the farmer receives consistently about one half the retail price. For instance, in 1969 the farmer received 27.6 cents per one half gallon. Home-delivered, this milk cost the consumer 62.3 cents, and 55.1 cents in stores. Inspection under highly sanitary standards, hauling, and retail profits accounted for about one half the price to the consumer. For her original part in the transaction, the cow received nothing.

Man is a carnivorous animal. He kills and eats other animals. Flesh, fish, and fowl are as much a part of his diet as fruits and vegetables, milk, butter, cheese, and eggs.

The total dressed weight of meat animals processed by meatpackers in 1968 was 34.6 billion pounds, an all-time record. This meant the slaughter of 31.5 million cattle, 4.15 million calves,

11.4 million sheep and lambs, and 70.4 million hogs—a total live weight of 53.37 billion pounds. When they get this large, figures become almost meaningless, but they give some idea of the consumption of meat in the United States.

Beef is the favorite meat of Americans, and the Bos ("Bossy" as a diminutive for cow comes from *Bos*, the family name of all wild and domesticated cattle) has been serving man for countless centuries. It was first an animal hunted like the bison, then domesticated as cows and oxen, then raised and herded as a meat animal. The first cattle are said to have been brought to the Western Hemisphere by Eric the Red in 982. Columbus brought an Andalusian bull and heifers. Hernando Cortez brought Andalusian cattle to Mexico in the sixteenth century to feed his armies and provide leather.

Americans now consume about a hundred pounds of beef per capita every year. Ranchers, farmers, feeders, commission men, and countless others, including bankers who finance land, herd, and equipment, chemists who make insecticides and pesticides, and pilots who spray ranges and fields, are involved in the marketing of beef. They are at work before the herd disappears into the stockyards, then into the packing plants, to come out as carcasses. These are shipped across the country and reach the consumer as steaks, roasts, tongue, liver, briskets, ground meat, or other cuts. Other parts of the animal are transformed into hides, gelatin, chemicals, and animal feed.

A thousand-pound steer produces 590 pounds of beef. Bone, fat, waste, and shrinkage leave about 465 pounds of this for retail cuts. Slaughtering and packing are done under strict government supervision, and meats are graded from top to bottom by the USDA as: prime, choice, good, standard, commercial, and utility. This grading ensures that the purchaser obtains the quality he desires, and it helps determine the price. Not only beef but all meats and poultry are inspected and graded by the United States Department of Agriculture in what is one of its most important services to the consumer.

As everyone knows, the retail prices of meat have skyrocketed in recent years, yet profits accruing to the rancher and the packer and to others in marketing meat until it reaches the the consumer buys, increased labor costs all along the line are generally responsible. In the meat-packing industry, wage and salary payments increased $120 million in 1968 over 1967. With other employee benefits, they accounted for more than half of all consumer are small. As with the prices of almost everything else operating expenses. Meat-packing returns a profit of only one percent on total sales in contrast to a return of 9.5 percent in drugs and medicine, where profits are highest, and 7.4 percent in soft drinks. At the retail level the scarcity of meatcutters has resulted in high butcher wages, adding to the consumer cost of meat.

Most of the advertising of unprocessed foods is at the local level; full pages of newspaper advertising by retail food markets shout of specials, bargains, and price advantages in cuts of meat and in canned goods. Food stores beg to give away larger trading stamps in prettier colors with better-tasting glue. There are branded apples, oranges, and other fruits advertised in national media, and trade associations push their products: eat more meat, apples, walnuts, oranges—drink more milk—ice cream is good for you—you need more eggs. . . .

It is in processed and branded products that marketing to the consumer through insistent advertising is marked. The various kinds of coffee, all superior, cereals that make you stronger, more handsome, and energy-charged, branded meat specialties such as frankfurters, hams, or sausages, patented diet foods—all these are pushed hard. Branded dairy products, cheese spreads, and the like are touted. Sauces and condiments are sprinkled all over television programs. Canned soup has been insistently and successfully advertised for more than a half century, and canned beans, corn, sliced peaches, tuna fish, and countless other items are equally heavily advertised, so that most people know the names of the leading brands. They are not allowed to forget them.

Their packages are familiar as you push a cart through the

aisles of your market. Sight of the package makes your taste buds remember, and you buy. People need not be urged to eat and drink, but marketing can persuade them to drink this rather than that, spread this cheese mix rather than a competitor's, sniff the aroma of this advertised bacon rather than chance a rasher of some unbranded side. When this little pig goes to market, he seldom goes as in the nursery rhyme. He goes as bacon, pork, ham, sausage, even cortisone, a drug used in the treatment of arthritis.

There really is a difference among some processed and branded foods. The sausage called a frankfurter, wiener, hot dog, or any other name originated in Austria or Germany perhaps as early as the thirteenth century, but it is Americans who eat most of them now. According to the American Meat Institute, about 1.5 billion pounds of frankfurters are made here every year— about eighty frankfurters for every individual in the United States. Frankfurters are made of chopped and ground meat and spices forced into cellulose or natural containers which are then cooked in huge ovens where smoke produces the flavor and the dark-red color. Some are then steamed or cooked in hot water.

Frankfurters may all look the same, but they are not. Made under USDA inspection, they are labeled and stamped. The "all meat" label means that they contain meat, usually beef and pork, with added seasonings but no filler. The label "frank-furters" on a package does not indicate that the contents are all meat. They contain seasonings plus a filler such as milk powder and soy-bean flour. The "all beef" frankfurter is just that. The sausage contains no other meat or filler. The Kosher label means that these all-beef frankfurters have been processed, like other Kosher meats, under the added supervision of rabbis.

With frankfurters, as with many other products, the brand name under which they are marketed may well make a difference in quality and nutritional value as well as in taste.

Manufacturers and national distributors of processed and

branded food products are among the heaviest advertisers. The General Foods Corporation, with headquarters in White Plains, just outside the city of New York, offers about seventy-five principal branded food products to the consumer; most of them are for people, but some of them are for pets. It processes and distributes coffees, other beverages, packaged desserts, cereals, quick-frozen foods, baking products, and many grocery items. The names of many GF brands are household words: Jell-O, Grape-Nuts, Postum, Maxwell House, Birds-Eye, Sanka, Post Toasties, Baker's Chocolate, Gaines Meal, Gravy Train, Gaines-burgers, Top Choice. . . .

The total market for packaged desserts in the United States is estimated to be around $270 million annually. The market for ready-to-eat cereals is nearly $700 million—and that for pet foods is the same. General Foods has a large share of these and of the coffee market, and is continually striving to increase its share in all its product categories.

General Foods, whose net sales totaled more than $1.8 billion in fiscal 1969, spends millions upon millions every year to advertise its wares. One or another of its products is advertised on television almost anytime you turn on your set. That this tremendous advertising expenditure—plus satisfactory consumer experience with GF products—is effective is shown by the corporation's sales. Every shopping day, GF says, American consumers purchase twenty million packages of General Foods products sold under its major brand names.

Advertising of this kind and extent is necessary in the marketing of packaged and branded food products because of the change in people's shopping habits which has taken place in recent years.

— 11 —

Chain Store Marketing

For most of the first quarter of the twentieth century people walked to the village or neighborhood store to buy foods, hardware, and other convenience goods. When they needed to make larger purchases they went downtown if they lived in a city, or to the nearest town if they lived in smaller places or in the country.

One block on Third Avenue in South Brooklyn, for instance, had, side by side, a grocer's, a butcher's, a barber's, a bakery, a drugstore, and a stationer's. On every corner there was a saloon and across the street was a neighborhood department (or dry-goods) store. These took care of most of the daily needs of families in the vicinity. If someone wanted an icebox, a bedroom suite, a stove, or comparable heavier and more expensive articles, he took the trolley car, the elevated train, or the new subway and went to downtown Brooklyn, where there were large department stores on Fulton Street; or he took the ferry and went a little farther to Wanamaker's, Macy's, Siegal Cooper's, Lord & Taylor's, Altman's, or Stern's in Manhattan.

When people did not walk to neighborhood or small-town stores, the store came to the house. The grocer's outside clerk came every morning to take the order. It was delivered in the afternoon and charged to the customer's account. Sometimes the grocer's man walked. The more fortunate drove a horse and buggy, later a runabout, and covered a larger territory.

The telephone, cash-and-carry chain stores, the automobile, supermarkets, shopping plazas, and self-service changed all this to family marketing as we know it today.

Local independent merchants were the rule early in this century. They predominate still, but the chain store is the familiar phenomenon of contemporary life. There are grocery chains, variety-store chains, drug chains, hardware chains, the chain stores of the big mail-order houses, and discount-store chains.

George Huntington Hartford from Augusta, Maine, was working with George F. Gilman in the hide and leather business in New York when he persuaded Gilman that tea, then selling for a dollar a pound, could be sold for thirty cents by dispensing with jobbers and wholesalers. The two men formed the Great American Tea Company and opened a store on Vesey Street in New York in 1859. It looked more like P. T. Barnum's American Museum.

Over the red store was a huge, gaslit capital letter "T." There were strings of red, white, and blue globes. The cashier's cage was built to resemble a Chinese pagoda. Hartford and Gilman sold their tea cheaply and packed in the customers by giving away premiums of tinware and crockery. An eight-horse team hauled a huge red wagon through the New York streets, and the two new tea merchants offered twenty thousand dollars to anyone who could guess the correct weight of the horses and wagon. This was the kind of showmanship not only Barnum but later Sir Thomas Lipton used to sell his dairy products, pork and bacon, and then his tea. Early in his career Lipton had worked for several years as a grocery clerk in New York. People loved the excitement provided by the Great American Tea Company, and they liked getting their tea for much less than they had been accustomed to pay.

Hartford and Gilman added spices, extracts, coffee, soap, baking powder, and condensed milk to their stock. They opened branch stores. They sold so much and made such profits that in 1869 they changed the name of their enterprise to The Great Atlantic and Pacific Tea Company, or A. & P., and Hartford planned A. & P. stores across the country. By 1876 there were seventy-six of these stores, all with the same red-and-gold fronts and each of them a complete grocery store selling a full line. The stores were manned by managers and clerks who waited on the customers. The A. & P. delivered groceries to the home, as the independents did, and carried charge accounts.

Gilman retired wealthy. George Huntington Hartford was joined in the business by his two sons, George and John. By 1880 the Hartfords had 110 stores. The A. & P. not only bought directly from producers, but also began to manufacture some of its own products. In a day when women baked the bread for their families, they started by making and selling their own baking powder.

When he assumed control of the operation in 1912, John Hartford introduced the A. & P. cash-and-carry policy. This did away with expensive bookkeeping. He opened more stores, red-and-gold bargain stores each operated by one man. There were a thousand A. & P. stores by 1915. All looked alike. Stock was arranged the same way in each, so that customers could easily find what they wanted. The founding Hartford died in 1917, aged eighty-four, leaving a grocery empire that continued to expand in size, sales, profit, and favor with the public. By 1925 there were 14,034 red-fronted stores of The Great Atlantic and Pacific Tea Company. Justifying the grandiose name assumed sixty-one years before, there were 15,737 of them by 1930, when for the first time sales topped one billion dollars for the year. By this time The Atlantic and Pacific was processing its own foods under its own labels in its own plants scattered across the country.

Chain stores opened in other lines. Frank W. Woolworth opened his first five-and-ten-cent variety store on a side street in Utica, New York, in 1879. His was the first of many variety chains. By the middle of the twentieth century there were nearly two thousand Woolworth stores—with prices no longer limited to five and ten cents—in the United States and Canada, another eight hundred or so in a British Woolworth company, and a half hundred in Germany.

Like the A. & P., Woolworth soon had competition—from the chains of J. G. McCrory, S. S. Kresge, W. T. Grant, J. J. Newberry, and others. Where once they had had an individuality lent them by the presence of independent stores, the Main Streets of American towns all began to look alike—the same chain grocery and variety stores, gasoline stations, and Montgomery Ward and Sears, Roebuck stores.

As the chains engendered their own competition they also provoked strong and organized opposition from outside. Emotionally, people disliked them. They were intruders in the community. They could underbuy and undersell local shops. Many people considered it their duty to hate the chains, but they continued to buy from them, making their purchases where they could get the quality they wanted at bargain prices. Independent grocers banded against the grocery chains in a national association and pressed for government action to curb them.

All the chains drove hard bargains with their suppliers in order to buy at low cost in great quantities, then sell in huge volume at low cost to the consumer. On complaints instigated by the independents, a few chain store managers were convicted of selling short weight. Agitation for punitive taxes against the chains was started. Efforts to curtail them mounted in the 1920's. An act was proposed in Congress that prohibited advertising allowances by manufacturers except on the same terms to all buyers and forbidding discounts for quantity purchase except where these could be proved to give actual savings to the seller. A federal tax severe enough to put many chains out of business was demanded.

By 1929 there were 807 grocery chains with 54,000 stores, which accounted for more than 20 percent of all retail grocery sales. The independent grocers did not like this, but consumers reveled in the competition that reduced prices. The independents accused the chains of unfair buying practices from some 23,000 suppliers. As the Federal Trade Commission (FTC) discovered when it investigated, the chains got lower prices by buying in huge quantities and obtained the discounts granted large buyers, but that was all. The net profit of the grocery chains in 1929 was only 2.63 percent of sales. It was volume that brought in the profit.

The Great Atlantic and Pacific Tea Company fought back against the attackers. It took its case to the public in full pages of explanatory newspaper advertising. Concessions made to the chains were not due to illegal acts but to large-scale buying, keen market sense, and sharp competition. By use of their own brands, products processed and packaged to their specifications, the chains could market food items to the public at an average of 10 percent less in price than nationally advertised brands. The FTC found that manufacturers fared well in dealing with the grocery chains, both in manufacturing for them and in having a strong, sustained market for their own brands. As a result of its findings and the A. & P. advertising, the most repressive measures against the grocery chains were killed—but the battle was not over.

The Atlantic and Pacific was too big, and government suspects size that may lead to monopoly. Antitrust charges were filed against The Great Atlantic and Pacific Tea Company. It was found guilty and paid fines totaling $175,000. The Department of Justice then demanded separation of A. & P. manufacturing and retailing operations and the splitting of its retailing into several companies. This case never came to trial. The A. & P. successfully defended itself in a later antitrust action brought against it and its very successful *Woman's Day*. After it had won, the company divested itself of the magazine in 1957—evidently to avoid further difficulty.

The independents won part of their battle against the chain grocery stores. Between 1927 and 1960, twenty-eight states placed special license taxes on chain stores, threatening their existence, but this repressive measure was ineffective. In the end, it is generally the consumer who decides major marketing issues. Through their heavy patronage the public showed approval of the chain stores. More than half the states which had levied the taxes repealed the laws.

Just as the independent grocers put organized pressure on successful chain competition, the independent druggists—more strongly organized and more militant—attacked the drug chains. Drugstore markups are generally high on both drug and other products. Most people do not know much about drugs. They have to trust the druggist. Because of this, they pay for prescriptions without complaint. Independent druggists managed so that they all charged about the same for prescriptions and standard remedies. They sold at retail markups which were usually about 50 percent over cost to them. Using private brands, the chain drugstores charged the same as the independents and took much higher markups—some as high, it was reported, as 170 percent. The chains could undercut independent drugstore prices on many other name-branded items and still make large profits.

What the druggists managed to do was get manufacturers to draw up contracts binding all retailers to fixed prices on many items carried in drugstore inventories. These became the so-called state, then federal, Fair Trade laws. Despite the fierceness of their attack, the independents got little else. Once more, in effect, the chains won.

Meanwhile, great changes in retail marketing were taking place. Principal among them were self-service and the supermarket.

Where once customers were waited on by clerks in grocery and butcher shops, in variety and other stores, they now wait upon themselves. Transactions are impersonal. They are as little affected by human conversation and merchandise is as nearly untouched by human hands as economy of store operation and economy of consumer buying can make them. Usually the only employee the shopper deals with is the cashier at the checkout counter, and even there the transaction may be completed without talk. Grocery shopping in particular has become almost automated.

The Piggly Wiggly Corporation was a pioneer in self-service in grocery stores. There were already 2,800 stores operating under its franchise when the Piggly Wiggly president said (in *Chain Store Age*, September, 1932):

> . . . there's no one to delay you when you're in a hurry. There's no one rushing you when you want to stop and look. In these friendly, orderly aisles, you see all the familiar names you know and like—on cans and bottles and boxes. Here you find all similar products grouped together—so you can compare brands, and weights, and prices. Here is everything you want and need. . . . All arranged for quick and easy self-service.

This was Piggly Wiggly advertising, but the appeal of self-service was the same in other stores. The self-service idea spread during the Depression of the 1930's. People looked for bargains. The stores could operate with fewer employees. Customers got used to waiting on themselves and liked it.

The supermarket, which originated in New Jersey and Maryland, was also an outgrowth of the Depression. Many people were jobless. Few had much money, and many had almost none. Price was of paramount importance in buying necessities, and people bought few if any luxuries. The first supermarkets were just warehouses, even old carbarns. Goods purchased in bulk were tumbled into them, sold at cut rates, and people were glad to get them. Those first supermarkets sold only packaged foods. They began to sell meat, then to stock standard drug items, then many nonfood products. Customers felt they were buying at wholesale prices. The supermarkets became bigger and shinier as people crowded to them. Today the supermarket dominates the grocery and sundries scene.

The chrome-plated supermarket shopping cart is one of the

most familiar symbols of contemporary American life. The carts are wheeled through crowded aisles between shelves and stands of foods and other household items by aged men and women and by young housewives who often have a baby piled in among the canned goods, cellophane-wrapped cuts of meat, fruits, and vegetables, and cardboard packs of beverages. The supermarket shopping cart is the modern baby carriage. Considered expendable by many customers, the carts, sometimes intact, litter the huge parking spaces in shopping plazas. They appear far from the supermarket, serving as trailers to the bicycles of small boys, and, where trains survive, can be found scattered along the railroad right-of-way. They can be found, usually with the baby removed, abandoned in almost any up-and-coming neighborhood.

Several factors have contributed to the rapid growth of the supermarket. Perhaps most important is the automobile. The car has outmoded cities. It is impossible to park, sometimes even to stop, an automobile in congested downtown areas. It has become dangerous to drive into a city anywhere. With the crime rate increasing hourly, your car and even your life may be in danger.

This same automobile has made suburban or outlying city areas accessible. The shopper can drive there and park her car. She has her car at hand to transport herself back home with the bags and cartons of stuffs she has purchased. The automobile has made possible the shopping plaza, often a number of them on the main highways surrounding centers of population. Many of these plazas have become, in effect, village shopping centers by themselves. A woman can buy food, clothing, and housewares; get her hair done; gossip with her friends; eat her lunch; and dent a fender all in one place and in one short trip.

The supermarket has become the super-supermart and in some instances the super-super-supermarket. It is no longer a bleak warehouse or a dingy carbarn, but an elaborate and gleaming retail palace with enticing shelves of every conceivable kind of packaged food, with toys, games, cleaning compounds, cosmetics, gloves, stockings, patented drug preparations, picture frames, and hundreds of other nonfood items. In fact, the giant supermarket is the old-fashioned country store all over again, the general store. Of course, it is much larger, and it is based on the marketing principle of one-stop shopping. Nylons, hamburger, car wax, toothbrushes, hair dyes . . . why go somewhere else? It is all here. Markups on food products are low. Markups on nonfood items are higher, enabling the supermarkets to show a larger margin of profit than they can show on their high-volume foods.

The Great Atlantic and Pacific Tea Company has many fewer stores now than it once had, but they are much larger. No longer one-man red-and-gold stores on busy streets, they are Georgian brick buildings with acres of floor space. First National, Safeway, Kroger, Stop and Shop, Winn-Dixie—you know the dominant chain in your area—the supermarkets are everywhere.

By definition of the Super Market Institute, a supermarket is a complete, departmentalized food store with a minimum sales volume of one million dollars a year and with at least its grocery department fully self-service. Members of the Institute operated a total of nearly thirteen thousand supermarkets with sales of a million dollars or more each at the beginning of 1970. Many supermarkets are much larger than the defined minimum, doing a business of three million dollars or more annually. Operating expenses, particularly labor, are high; markups on foods are low. Tremendous volume accounts for the profit.

The supermarkets belong to chains; their ownership is usually elsewhere, but they employ people in the communities where they are located. Despite self-service, which keeps the number of workers at a minimum, the supermarkets employ about 790,000 people in their retail and supporting activities. About half are full-time and half part-time workers.

Self-service has a definite influence on the marketing of the branded foods and other branded merchandise—thousands of brands in all—which the supermarkets sell.

There are no salesmen to recommend one can of pork and beans or one cake of soap or one bag of potato chips over another. The customer must be predisposed to purchase a given brand before she enters the store. She must be presold, so that when she recognizes the color, shape, and trade name of a product, she reaches up and stows a package of it—rather than of a competing brand—in her shopping cart. Thus the unceasing din of national advertising for cereals, processed meats, pet foods, baked goods, canned fruits, and other goodies.

Because there is no personal selling in supermarkets, advertising has to be expanded, emphatic, and continuous. It is this that makes every new and improved brand of detergent washing powder with pink polyhedrons or green pollywog chips added ten times as good as yesterday's new and improved package that had only essence of peacock feathers and some merely secret alchemy which gave it magical properties. The manufacturers try to wash competing brands down the drain—even advertise competitively a half dozen brands of their own in order to get the largest possible share of the market through sales of them all.

In the mass marketing of groceries and the nongrocery items that people buy every day or two, self-service and the supermarket have taken over from the customer service and the single store. One-stop shopping has supplanted multiple-stop shopping; and national advertising has taken the place of personal selling.

Chain-store merchandising started in grocery marketing. It spread to the marketing of low-cost variety goods. It has expanded into other marketing areas.

— 12 —

Department Store Marketing: Federated

A department store is, naturally, a store with many departments, but that is only the beginning. A department store is a fair, a continual bazaar, a wealth of treasures. It is excitement and entertainment. It is part of growing up, for it is where Santa Claus is, and there are more shining toys than a child can dream of. It is where young men buy engagement rings, where brides shop for their trousseaux, where the newly married choose their furniture. The middle-aged shop for luxuries they could not afford when they were young, and the elderly return to replace a worn oriental rug or to buy a new electric range to take the place of the kitchen stove once bought there which has served them for most of a lifetime.

A department store is a place where people meet. It is a city landmark. It is the delight of spending money and the occasional joy of a bargain. Tradition and sentiment grow up about a department store over the years. It can be one of the pleasantest things ever a woman can have, and she returns to it again and again with anticipation—sometimes with the savage intent to snatch a bargain wig, a piano, or earrings marked down from eighty-nine to thirty-six cents before any other woman can snatch them from her.

F. & R. Lazarus, in Columbus, Ohio, was an old and well-known department store of this kind. Abraham & Straus, in downtown Brooklyn, was another. In Boston, Filene's was as well-known as the Bunker Hill Monument and better patronized. Its bargain basement was and is a New England institution. Shillito's, in Cincinnati, was comparable to the others in age, size, and traditions. It, too, had been in operation for several generations.

The owners and executives of these four stores knew each other well and had often worked together. In 1929 the stores were joined to form Federated Department Stores, Inc. Fred Lazarus, Jr., whose grandfather Simon Lazarus had founded the Columbus store, was the prime mover in this union to pool buying and selling resources, get geographical diversification, and intensify an exchange of information so that each of the four stores could learn from the successes and failures of the others.

All four had been family-owned stores, long established, of high repute. Founded by William Filene and carried on by his sons Lincoln and Edward, Filene's was the dominant Boston department store. Edward Filene became the great merchant, applying principles of scientific store management, interested in the welfare of his employees, and a student of world economics. The heads of the other three stores were also men of stature in business and in public affairs, but all of them were first of all merchants, retail marketers.

The four original stores were soon joined by big Bloomingdale's, one of the busiest stops along the East Side's crowded Lexington Avenue subway in New York. Federated did not start from nothing, and, goaded and guided by Fred Lazarus, Jr., it has become the biggest something in department store and allied marketing in the United States.

The planned growth of Federated Department Stores, Inc., was rapid from the first but especially marked after the end of World War Two and the long Depression which had preceded it. Federated bought Foley's in Houston, Texas, in 1945; Halliburton's in Oklahoma City in 1947; Sanger of Dallas in 1951. In 1953–1954 it opened eight new Fedway department stores in Texas, New Mexico, and California. It moved into Florida in 1960 through purchase of Burdine's with its three stores in the Miami area, one in Fort Lauderdale, and one in West Palm Beach. Federated bought Bullock's in Los Angeles, I. Magnin & Co. in San Francisco, Levy's in Tucson, and Rike's in Dayton. This was a good beginning—but tomorrow the world!

Federated did not stop. It was slowed a little by the Federal Trade Commission which, after a long investigation, issued a consent decree in 1965 but forbade it to acquire any more department stores for five years, or until August, 1970. The decree did not forbid extension of the department stores Federated already owned through construction of branches or Federated's entrance into other forms of retail marketing.

The discount store is a retail marketing outlet which has come to the fore since World War Two. Originally, many discount stores were (purportedly, at any rate) for the exclusive convenience of the members of a union or other associations whose members carried cards admitting them to purchase. This device fell away, and the discount stores, so to speak, went public. They sell or claim to sell at prices below those charged by the regular stores. They stock nationally branded merchandise, but also large quantities of inexpensive, often cheap, goods, in unadorned structures, many of which still resemble the first supermarkets. There are no organs and no fountains. Instead, there are bare walls, self-service, and racks and racks and counters and counters of clothes and household goods. There are durables that sometimes prove nondurable and quantities of quickly expendable soft goods. All the dignity and often the aesthetic appeal of the department store has been cut away. The whole appeal is to price or, as the discount stores advertise, to "value."

Subtle decor would be offensive to the kind of clientele the discount stores seek to attract or to shoppers in what might be called a discount-store mood. The bargain hunter does not need soft lights or soothing music. Discount-store patrons prefer the loudspeaker with, "Attention! Attention! For the next eleven minutes only, at Counter Ten, electric back scratchers will be sold at a fraction of their cost! Walk, run, or gallop to Counter Ten! For the next eleven minutes only, these marvelous itch ticklers which sell anywhere for twice the price will be sold for less than half! Attention! Attention! For the next eleven . . ."

There *are* bargains to be got in these discount stores which mass-market mass-produced and, sometimes, distress merchandise. You can get something "as is" for half price or less. You can also get surprised. A young doctor in Philadelphia was delighted with the sports coat of excellent British tweed, well tailored, which he had seized on in the nearest outlet of a discount chain. He was proudly showing off its fit and quality when he reached to insert his thermometer and eyeglasses in its breast pocket. He fumbled several times in amazement, then consternation, before he was convinced. There was no breast pocket. Someone had made a mistake. The coat could not pass routine factory inspection, so to the discounters it went.

At the urging of Fred Lazarus, Jr., Federated Department Stores inaugurated its Golden Circle discount chain, starting with stores in Columbus and Dayton and then moving into other cities. Federated planned and built them as superior to those generally known, providing better physical surroundings, offering salespersons as well as self-service, and stocking some fashion merchandise. It made its Golden Circle stores, in fact, more like department stores, though they sold soft goods only. Federated followed with Golden Triangle discount stores to sell major home appliances and other hard goods.

In 1967, Federated took the next indicated step. It purchased Ralphs Industries, a ninety-four year old company with a chain of fifty-four supermarkets, a creamery, a bakery, and a meat-processing plant in Los Angeles. Immediately it began to expand Ralphs. So far, it has added twelve more supermarkets to the Ralphs chain.

All of this determined expansion has produced figures so large that they convey only the idea of vastness, vast vastness. They are, anyway, only temporary figures, for Federated intends to change them, and its plans for future growth dwarf the growth already attained.

Federated Department Stores, Inc., has about one hundred department store units. It has sixteen operating divisions in sixty different places. It has about 25 million square feet of department-store selling space and almost 2 million more square feet of floor space in its discount stores and supermarkets. In 1969, Federated's net sales were nearly two billion dollars ($1.99 billion). Its earnings per share were $1.98—a good department store price. With more than nineteen hundred buyers, Federated had some twenty million sales transactions in its stores during the year.

Bullock's has nine branches; I. Magnin has twenty; Foley's has four; Sanger-Harris, six; Bloomingdale's, five; Abraham & Straus, six; Filene's, nine. By the time this book is printed, they and the other Federated department stores will have more branches, and new expansion will be taking place.

Shillito's has opened a store in Louisville, Kentucky, one hundred miles from Cincinnati, and will open another in Lexington in the Kentucky Bluegrass country. I. Magnin is jumping two thousand miles to open a store in Chicago. There may be a Filene's in Providence, Rhode Island. Lazarus will invade Mansfield, Ohio, and perhaps Detroit. Burdine's will open stores in other Florida cities, Orlando and St. Petersburg. New Bullock's branches will stretch from Santa Barbara to San Diego.

The marketing policy of Federated is simple. *Grow*. Take in more territory, sell to more people in more places. Increase profits. Federated goes in for long-range marketing plans, for personal service in its stores, for quality merchandise, and for both centralization and decentralization. That is, plans and policy are made in the Cincinnati headquarters, where sales goals and quotas are set, but each store is run by its own personnel on its own basis. Though it is a chain, Federated eschews the chain-store look or the chain-store attitudes. Their individuality is one of the most valuable assets of each of the big department stores in the chain, and Federated wants that individuality maintained.

There is no compulsory retirement at age sixty-five for entrepreneurs and top executives in most companies. When they are doing what they like to do and doing it well, they do not wish to retire, and their organizations generally do not wish them to. Fred Lazarus, Jr., who created Federated Department Stores, Inc., relinquished the chairmanship of the Federated board when he was eighty-two, but only to become chairman of its executive and finance committee. His son Ralph is now board chairman and chief corporate officer. Another son, Maurice, who headed Filene's for some years, is vice-chairman. Currently the president of Federated is J. Paul Sticht, brought in from Campbell Soup in 1960. At Campbell's he had practiced national marketing at the manufacturing level. There are four group presidents at Federated and three executive vice-presidents. One of these is Robert M. Fuoss, who, as last editor of the powerful *Saturday Evening Post* when it was still a weekly magazine, knew how to reach the mass markets of millions of readers who are also consumers.

Federated markets fashion merchandise. It believes in fashion and the steady profit in it.

During the early fifties, men wore wide, flowing, four-in-hand neckties. Suddenly they were passé, and a man with any self-respect dared not be seen in any but a narrow tie. They got narrower and narrower until the approved necktie looked rather like a single lonely horsehair. That was enough. As suddenly as they had vanished, wide neckties came back, wider than ever. A man careful of his image dares not be seen in anything but a wide necktie patterned as loudly as his conscience will permit. The narrow tie marks the reactionary, the square, the not-with-it clown. Tomorrow? The cravat may come back, or even the ruff. Perhaps there'll be no necktie at all, a growing affectation. Because men are like sheep (the truth of the matter is that sheep are like men), they will all wear the same thing. This does not annoy manufacturers, distributors, and retailers of men's neckwear at all. One market disappears, and another, more profitable one, appears.

Lapels on men's suits go from almost nothing to those which seem to span the distance from the breastbone to the shoulder. The double-breasted suit was supplanted by the single-breasted suit which has been supplanted by what looks like the double-double-breasted suit. Skintight jeans are in and baggy pants are out or *vice versa,* and bellbottoms are with us or they are not. Trousers have cuffs, and then they don't, and then they do. The white shirt becomes the crimson pink or the purple stripes with orange checks and green polka dots—then it is the bleached white shirt again. These vagaries are known as fashion. If they are this marked with the timid male, they know no bounds with the far-from-timid female.

A look around is all anyone needs to see hemline and neckline trying to coincide, while the cold-weather coverall hides the microskirt by sweeping the sidewalk. Spiked heels collapse to heellessness or stretch into knee boots. Nylon stockings become leotard encasements. At the moment, nudity is winning the battle with modesty, but the flowing medieval robe with snood and coif or the Elizabethan stomacher may be just around the corner again. Pretty confusion at the display of an ankle may return and replace the carefree exhibition of most of the body's bones and the flesh that holds them together.

Fashion is unpredictable. Like the stock market, it will fluctuate, but it will always be there. Women's fashion is a market worth $83 billion a year, and Federated lives happily in the midst of it.

Most women wear shoes. In the United States they buy $2.5 billion worth of shoes at retail every year. They usually don't wear out their shoes. They don't discard them, but they can't wear them any more. They are not what the television actresses, the *Vogue* models, or Judy O'Grady and the colonel's lady are wearing.

Federated believes that people no longer buy only what they need, but also, and perhaps even more, what it gives them pleasure to buy. Americans have money, they like to spend it, and Federated is there to help them. Federated believes that as people become more and more affluent, they will be willing to pay for personal service in department stores and enjoy having it. Missing no bets, the corporation works the other way in its discount or "value" stores. In these it offers less expensive merchandise and more bargains, but even in these stores it offers attractive surroundings and courteous service as well as the convenience of self-service—and fashion.

In 1968, a Federated executive told the Society of Security Analysts, "Making sure they can find it—when they want it, where they want it, and at prices they want to pay—is our business." In reality, this is the business of the whole of marketing.

Federated makes sure it knows what the consumer wants and will buy. The flow of information from all its stores to Cincinnati, then its release to other Federated stores, allows all to profit by the experience of one.

Many of its successful innovations are touched with marketing imagination. In Italy, an I. Magnin buyer saw a backless sandal and thought a comparable sandal would sell well in the United States. He had a model made here and sold 15,000 pairs at $20 retail for a volume of $300,000. A Federated stationery buyer saw colorful mobiles in Scandinavia. He bought 75,000 for the Christmas shopping season. Since they were hung, the mobiles took no floor space. People saw them, liked them, and bought in volume. A Federated men's clothing buyer liked the reverse side of a swatch of cloth shown him by a manufacturer of men's clothing. He dubbed it "Corrigan Twill" and placed a large order for suits made of the reversed material. Corrigan Twill became one of the most popular fabrics in the manufacturer's line.

Long well known for its home-furnishings department, Bloomingdale's developed its own designs for furniture to be manufactured both in the United States and abroad. It got a large American manufacturer to make a collection of French Provincial furniture based on its designs and finishes. More than ten million dollars' worth of it was sold.

Again in Bloomingdale's, a buyer of women's coats (he had played end at the University of Arizona) saw in Paris a full-length women's coat which he thought would sell well. He bought 125 of them, some single and some double-breasted, in various colors. On their first showing in New York in the summer of 1968, 38 of them were sold—with the temperature in Manhattan at 91 degrees. The buyer immediately ordered more.

By January, 1969, Bloomingdale's had sold maxicoats worth $90,000 at retail. Miniskirters became maxicoaters with a fierce determination as the style was imitated. The Bloomingdale buyer then bought maxicoats in suede and finished leather, fur-lined, from a source in Israel. By the end of 1969, Bloomingdale's had sold $110,000 worth of the Paris coats and $30,000 worth of the Israeli version.

Federated Department Stores, Inc., represents mammoth mass marketing on a national and even an international scale. In 1964 it bought a one-tenth interest—later reduced to one ninth —in Galerías Preciados, a leading department store in Spain. It has sold $20 million worth of Federated securities to finance further planned development abroad. Despite this vastness of operation, Federated avoids the impersonal in its merchandising, the automated and computerized atmosphere of the chain. It prides itself on its direct dealing with human problems and stresses the closeness of its relations to its customers.

Even before it went into supermarkets and value stores, Federated marketed some 275,000 to 300,000 different items. "What does Madam desire today, a packet of safety pins, a diamond tiara, a new glass top for her percolator, or a new wardrobe for the winter in Florida?" Add a few hundred thousand additional products carried in Ralphs supermarkets and in the Golden Circle and Golden Triangle stores. "Would Madam care for a case of canned peaches, a dozen rolls of paper towels, a refrigerator-freezer with a washer-and-dryer attachment?" The Extra Large USDA Grade AA Fancy Fresh eggs are just in from the farm, the evening gown from Paris, the gold brocade draperies after an eleventh-century Chinese pattern from Dalton, Georgia, and, yes, we do have bananas today.

There is a special on men's raincoats in Filene's basement, perhaps on rare jade in I. Magnin's. The sirloin tips are delicious today at Ralphs in Watts, and the Georgian breakfronts at Bloomingdale's are a find. The Ohio Yankee peddler carries a larger stock to a richer market than Bronson Alcott of Connecticut had in his two tin trunks.

In a way, Federated Department Stores, Inc., practices class marketing to the mass market. It does it everywhere, or so nearly everywhere as to make little difference. Tomorrow it will do it in even more places.

— 13 —

Class Marketing: Sea Pines Plantation

All of marketing is not mass marketing to achieve the widest-possible distribution of meats and branded grocery products or variety- or department-store items of frequent purchase at comparatively low cost. It is not even the mass marketing used to move automobiles or high-priced durable objects such as furniture and the major household appliances. It is not mass marketing at all.

In contrast, it is class marketing. It is used to bring ideas and large-scale actualities based on these ideas to a highly selective market.

What is bought and sold in these markets cannot be carried home in a shopping bag or delivered by parcel post or delivery service. It may be a large and complicated piece of textile machinery for which there are only a hundred possible customers in the world. It may be a larger and faster aircraft than any now in existence, with the possible prospects for it only national governments or the world's major airlines.

No one just goes ahead and makes such a piece of textile machinery or a high-speed, full-color printing press that costs at least a million dollars to build. No one just makes a huge airplane and then tries to market it. First the ideas behind these costly and still unproved contrivances must be sold.

They must be presented so convincingly and in such detail that a government, a corporation, a bank or group of banks believes they will work and will put up the money that makes construction possible. The idea of a huge dam, an atomic power plant, or some comparable project has to be marketed to investors before work on it can be started.

Corporations get the money to finance their original operation, and then expansion, in this way. They sell stocks—shares in their enterprises—to the public. People buy them in the belief that what the corporation makes is good, that it will get better, that sales will increase. Then they will get dividends on their investments, and the value of the stocks themselves will increase. In 1955, the Ford Motor Company, which had always been privately owned, decided to sell seven million shares. It offered this stock through a syndicate of seven banking houses in January, 1956. All of the stock was sold immediately, mostly through advance sales, and Ford obtained $642 million in new working capital to finance the manufacture of the various models of Ford cars and other Ford products.

Large-scale real estate developments have to be financed. There is no original marketing involved when these are government projects. Tax money is appropriated for slum clearance, urban renewal, public housing, and the like. The government —city, state, federal, or a combination—underwrites the work and construction is contracted out, usually to the lowest bidder.

Private real estate development does have to be marketed. The developer has to sell banks and other investors on the practicality and profitability of the plan before he can uproot the first tree. Once financing has been obtained, bulldozers roar in and mow down everything in sight: old houses, roads, oaks, pines, robins' nests, and cemetery markers. They level off the hills and fill the valleys.

Then the oceans of cement are poured and acres of cinder blocks mortared. High-rise apartments shoot up, or long rows of two-story garden apartments, every one of them the same, mushroom into being. An industrial complex with office buildings and a multistoried garage springs up in what had been a farmer's field or the town dump. A row of stores and a dozen houses disappear and, lo!, a new shopping plaza even larger and more elaborate than the one a hundred yards down the road. Instant towns have been built in this way. Levittown on Long Island, New York, and Levittown, New Jersey, are well known. A complete small city named Columbia is being created between Washington, D. C., and Baltimore, Maryland. Begun in 1966, it is expected to be completed by 1980. Most people are familiar with real estate development of this kind, ranging from the bare and purely utilitarian to the more pretentious.

Sometimes the controlling concept behind the creation of a place is different, and the creation is different. One such major real estate development is unique and provides a unique example of large-scale class marketing.

Early in the sixteenth century the Spanish landed on a large, deeply forested island off the Atlantic Coast on what became the southeastern corner of South Carolina. Piously they named it first Punta de Santa Elena, but after more practical experience with it changed the name to La Isla de los Osos, or "island of the bears." The French, who came about the same time, disputed the Spaniards for possession. As happened often in the early history of North America, the English took it from them both.

In August, 1663, Captain William Hilton, master of the *Adventurer,* out of Gravesend, England, sailed up from Barbados and, just above what would someday be Savannah, Georgia, sighted the island. He was impressed by its greenness, the tall pines, and the sweet air. In his ship's log he wrote that the island was "the goodliest, best, and frutefullest that ever was seen."

This was the English discovery of Hilton Head Island, the largest Atlantic Coast island in the United States, after Long Island, New York. As part of South Carolina, it developed during colonial times and up to the Civil War as cotton country. Choice sea-island long-staple cotton was grown on plantations with their mansions and their quarters for the slaves who were originally imported from Barbados and the West Indies. They were voodooists, speaking the melodious Gullah, a mixture of African and English. Its tones can still be heard on Hilton Head Island.

The Civil War put an end to the plantations and the cotton. Because it commanded Port Royal Sound, Fort Walker on Hilton Head was of strategic importance. Federal troops attacked, seized it, and turned Hilton Head into a great Union headquarters and a naval coaling station for ships blockading the Confederacy. There were tens of thousands of men stationed on Hilton Head Island in a city of earthworks, tents, and frame houses that had its hotels, restaurants, a theater, and even two newspapers. For three and a half years it was a busy military installation.

Hilton Head was virtually deserted after the Civil War. There were a few farms and houses, the remains of its plantations, but mostly it reverted to its tall pines, rustling palmettos, and deep swamplands. The official guide to South Carolina published by the Works Progress Administration in 1941 gave two paragraphs to Hilton Head's history but, except for mention of the Hilton Head raccoon, which is found nowhere else in the world, no space at all to the island's present. It had none in 1941. The small farms of local black families were the only clearings in a wilderness used as a hunting preserve by two New York families.

In 1949, Joseph B. Fraser, president of the Fraser Lumber Company of Hinesville, Georgia, and a National Guard officer who retired as a lieutenant general in 1956 after service in three wars, purchased from the New York interests for $450,000 an 8,000-acre tract at the southern tip of the island. While he was on active duty in the Korean War, associates in the Hilton Head Company obtained another 12,000 acres of the island's total of 27,000. After the mature pine had been harvested except along the water front, General Fraser exchanged his 51 percent interest in this company for half of the original 8,000-acre land purchase.

A ferry was established between Hilton Head Island and the

South Carolina mainland in 1953. It was supplanted in 1956 by the James F. Byrnes bridge. In 1957, twenty-seven-year-old Charles Elbert Fraser and his older brother, Joseph B. Fraser, Jr., purchased the 4,000 acres from their family. The purchase price was $500,000, payable over ten years. They then bought from the Hilton Head Company an adjacent 1,200 acres for $1.1 million, payable over twenty years at a low interest rate. Thus the Sea Pines Plantation Company, holding the southernmost 5,200 acres of ocean-edged forest, was formed, with General Fraser as chairman of the board and Charles E. Fraser as president and chief executive officer.

Born in tiny Hinesville in south Georgia in 1929, Charles E. Fraser attended a small Presbyterian College in Clinton, South Carolina, of which his father was chairman of the board of trustees. He transferred to the School of Business of the University of Georgia in Athens, graduating in 1950. He took a law degree from Yale in 1953 and was admitted to the Georgia bar. For one year, 1953–1954, he practiced in Augusta, then served in Washington for two years as a legal affairs lieutenant in the Office of the Secretary of the Air Force.

Fraser had spent one summer on Hilton Head. He liked it, and he had one basic idea. He wished to develop Sea Pines Plantation on its southern tip as a quality residential and resort community.

General Fraser backed his sons' notes for $80,000, needed for primary research and market planning. A textile-mill owner invested $100,000 in Hilton Head land and then organized a partnership to finance the island's first golf course. More working capital was obtained through the sale of the first lots in the eight square miles of Sea Pines Plantation. Holding 83 percent of the stock (his brother had the remaining shares), Charles Fraser gathered a working staff of hard-headed young visionaries about him and went to work.

Resorts spring up overnight. Lots are sold in subdivisions that have not yet been laid out. Lakefront properties are advertised in superlatives before the lake exists or is only a mud puddle with a bulldozer or two mired in it. Oceanfront lots have been sold while they were still under water. Beautiful shorelines have been completely despoiled by all the paraphernalia of honky-tonk and the refuse-spewing crowds they attract.

Fraser wanted none of this. He had an unspoiled wilderness of pine and palm. He had four miles of straight wide beach, the white sand packed so hard that a man can walk on it without leaving a footprint. The Atlantic slopes gently away from Hilton Head. The surf is gentle, the water clear and clean, the air as sweet as when Captain Hilton breathed it.

Fraser wanted to accomplish two ends that have generally been found antagonistic: to build a community of good contemporary homes, air-conditioned and hurricane-resistant; and to practice rigid conservation that would retain the natural beauty of the heavily wooded island. To realize these objectives, he could not exploit Hilton Head. He had to have a master plan for development and then a means of inaugurating and maintaining tight control over its every phase. Above all, he had to have a market for what he had to sell.

Intensive, extensive (and expensive) marketing research defined the primary market for Fraser and his associates. The kind of community they visualized can go only to an affluent market. They decided that Sea Pines Plantation, aesthetic standards impeccable, would be built for and its appeal directed to those with minimum annual incomes of $25,000. No maximum was set. Only a small percentage of the population was in this upper income group in 1957, but the percentage was growing every year. Quality standards were ensured in the basic planning.

The land-use plan for the building of Sea Pines Plantation was drawn up by the Watertown, Massachusetts, firm of landscape architects headed by Hideo Sasaki, chairman of the department of landscape architecture at Harvard. Myres S. McDougal, Sterling Professor of Law at Yale, strongly influenced Fraser's concept of special deed covenants under which homesites are sold and houses built on them.

Under terms of this plan and the covenant deeds, Sea Pines

Plantation set aside one quarter of its domain, two of its eight square miles, to be retained in perpetuity as undeveloped wilderness so managed as to preserve the flora and maintain a balanced wildlife population. The beach and sand dunes are held in permanent trust by the company. There are no buildings on them, and no homes are visible alongside. They are recessed in the woods.

The minimum initial price set by the company, for a house to be built in Sea Pines was $25,000, exclusive of the land cost. Few, if any, have been built for that amount. The lowest average price now is probably between $35,000 and $45,000. Some have cost over $200,000; at least one, $250,000. However eminent the architect—and almost all Sea Pines homes are designed by professional architects—the plans must be submitted to the company's architectural review committee, which has rejected some for purely aesthetic reasons. Lots, all heavily wooded, sell, depending upon location, from perhaps $10,000 to over $50,000. Some face the ocean; some face Calibogue Sound, toward the mainland; some face one of the three golf courses; and others are on lagoons or inland waterways. If and when a house comes up for sale, the Sea Pines Plantation Company reserves the right to buy it at the price offered by any private bidder. The company handles the rentals of houses if owners wish to let them during prolonged absence.

Fraser defined his market as national, well-to-do, well informed, and sophisticated. It is to these he has successfully marketed his idea and its implementation.

Most Sea Pines homes are of bleached cypress, a silver gray that seems as natural as the undersides of leaves in the wind before a rain. They are built in clusters on private roads with walkways to the water. Everything about Sea Pines Plantation is reserved, discreet, and unobtrusive. There is no ostentation, just quiet worth blending into the background of pine, palm, moss-draped water oak, magnolias, wild azalea, and hardwoods. There is privacy—one of the most expensive items on the contemporary menu. Thus far, people from some forty states and several foreign countries have found what they sought in Sea Pines Plantation and have built or bought there.

As homes were being built, so were the resort facilities: golf courses, marinas, riding stables, tennis courts. Just outside Sea Pines in the adjacent Forest Beach area are inns, a supermarket, a modern medical center, banks and brokerage offices, decorators' shops, and the other community necessities and amenities. Churches have been built on Hilton Head land donated by the Frasers.

The Plantation Club, which is owned by the Sea Pines Company, cost over $800,000 to build. Flanked by two eighteen-hole championship golf courses, this club is, in a way, the community center, but hardly of the ordinary kind. It is superbly equipped for golf. The decor is subdued elegance. Its dining room serves Carolina low-country dishes as well as international cuisine. Like the whole of Sea Pines, the Plantation Club is attractive, but only to those it would attract. The initiation fee for members who acquired their lots or properties from the Sea Pines Company is $400; for those who live outside the Plantation but within twenty-five miles it is $3,000. Annual dues and other charges are in proportion. On a temporary basis the club is open to vacationers renting homes from the company and to guests in its inn.

On the oceanfront, just outside the gates manned by guards which give Sea Pines Plantation the air of a residential park, is the 134-room Hilton Head Inn. This, too, is wholly owned by the Sea Pines Company. It contributes substantially to Sea Pines revenue. From all sources, the Sea Pines Plantation Company had total revenue in 1968 of $10,044,210. Its net income from this amount was $1,160,256.

In 1956 there was not one occupied dwelling on that southernmost part of Hilton Head Island which is Sea Pines Plantation. There was not an inhabitant except perhaps some Hilton Head raccoons. In 1970 there were more than six hundred homes belonging to the successful and sometimes eminent men and women who spend all or part of the year on the island.

Two kinds of marketing helped produce this result. The first was the marketing of the idea and the plans to financial institutions and private investors who might be induced to invest in a possibility and who provided the many millions of dollars needed to turn an idea into a reality. Its very uniqueness mitigated against the Sea Pines concept. Of necessity, the market was limited to the affluent, and even there it was limited. The boisterous millionaire would no more be attracted to the kind of residential and resort community Fraser planned than the penniless derelict.

The many restrictions which the company placed on home builders could be another hazard. The company even demanded that every home have a screened service area, and that plans for it, down to the kind of fencing proposed, be approved by its staff before it was built. House trailers and the like, Fraser said, would be "flatly rejected." His deliberate setting aside of 1,280 acres, which it might be possible to exploit for quick profit through lot sales, as a parklike wilderness also seemed a dubious move.

Fraser and his colleagues presented their case firmly. They prepared a ninety-page study, "Hilton Head Island: Economic Asset in the Regional Economy," and circulated it to banks and insurance companies. They made personal solicitations for investment funds. There were disappointments, numerous refusals, but the Sea Pines Company got the money because they proved their case to shrewd listeners.

By law, life-insurance companies are strictly regulated in the investment of their tremendous assets. The Travelers Insurance Company has invested many millions in Sea Pines Plantation. There are other heavy investors and many smaller ones. Underneath the Southern charm and elegance of Sea Pines Plantation there is a web of intricate financing and a business acumen that has no geographical limitation. The marketing to attract investment is continuous, but it is easier now. The Plantation itself is there to show, and substantiating facts are unarguable. Villas are sold for double or more than double their original price. Houses have increased in value by as much as half. An oceanfront lot which sold for $7,000 in 1957 will bring upward of $50,000 now. As someone noted a long time ago, nothing succeeds like success.

The marketing to prospective lot buyers, home builders, and residents was a different matter in 1957. Few people except those in the immediate vicinity had ever heard of Hilton Head Island, much less of Sea Pines Plantation. The wealthy who bought or built vacation or second homes or the well-to-do planning on retirement knew of Florida, Arizona, and other resort communities but not of Hilton Head.

This meant recourse to advertising and the seeking of all the favorable publicity possible. Sea Pines has its staff advertising and public-relations experts as well as its financial and architectural advisers. It uses an Atlanta advertising agency. The former marketing research director of The Curtis Publishing Company acts as its resident marketing consultant. Pamphlets and brochures describing the delights of Hilton Head were prepared. They described its favorable climate and scenery and the proposed golf, boating, and fishing facilities. These publications were sent to selected lists of prospects.

Advertising is paid publicity; publicity is unpaid advertising. Sea Pines worked to get that too. *Sports Illustrated, Realités, Fortune, Holiday,* and comparable nationally circulated periodicals said pleasant things about Sea Pines Plantation, and the company quoted their comments in its marketing effort. Invaluable publicity resulted when, only two years after formation of the Sea Pines Plantation Company, its master plan for the development of a resort community was awarded the Certificate of Excellence in Design of the American Society of Landscape Architects. Other awards followed. In 1969 Sea Pines Plantation received the first award by the American Institute of Architects of its Certificate of Excellence in Private Community Planning. As one commentator phrased it, Charles Fraser was shrewd enough to overestimate the taste of that part of the public which constitutes his market.

Principal marketing tool of Sea Pines Plantation now is its "Community Basic Data" booklet. Kept current through the issuance of new editions, this is a factual listing of the community's residential and resort advantages, with sales promotion kept to a minimum. Well illustrated, the booklet gives the prospective lot buyer the necessary information about average land and building costs, climate, state and county taxes (there are no city taxes), water, sewage disposal, electricity, schools and churches, and the rest. It lists fees and amounts payable to the Sea Pines Plantation Company for property and private-road maintenance, police patrol, and other services. "Community Basic Data" accomplishes its marketing objectives by the time-honored device of letting a proven product speak for itself.

In a reversal of the usual procedure, Sea Pines built its suburbs first. It is now building its town center. In a joint venture with The Travelers Insurance Company, which is investing $30 million in the Plantation, the first $7 million in this enterprise, a whole village was going up at once in the summer of 1970.

Hilton Head has long been a way-stop on the Intercoastal or Inland Waterway which stretches along the Atlantic coast from Maine to Florida. About seventy-five miles south of Charleston, an easy day's run for a small power boat, and forty-five miles north of Savannah, it has a natural harbor on Calibogue Sound. About it, the Lighthouse Beach Company (Travelers and Sea Pines) is building Harbour Town. The harbor dredged and enlarged to accommodate a hundred boats and guarded by a new ninety-foot lighthouse, Harbour Town, in contrast to the rest of Sea Pines Plantation, will be deliberately a sociably congested place.

One hundred and twenty-five acres in extent, it will be a port of call for yachtsmen, providing docks and anchorage and all the facilities skippers and crews could ask. In Harbour Town there will be 450 residential units: private town houses with walled gardens after the old Charleston manner, apartments, villas, condominiums. In two- to four-story Harbour House there will be offices, specialty shops, a restaurant, apartments, and artists' studios. Studies of tides and currents, ecological studies—and additional searching and detailed marketing studies—preceded start of construction on plans prepared by the same firm which created the master plan for Sea Pines Plantation.

The first golf club in the United States was organized in Charleston in 1786 as the South Carolina Golf Club. Revived and reorganized under a state charter, it is now the Harbour Town course. Two restored lighthouse-keeper houses, among the oldest intact buildings on Hilton Head, are in place and functioning. One is the Sea Pines office just off the village center. The other is the library for the newly formed Institute of Environmental and Leisure Studies.

Again in contrast to the rest of the Plantation, Harbour Town will be brightly and gaily colored, a compressed energy center. It is targeted at a new market. It reaches for private boat traffic, transient rather than resident, for those who see an opportunity for opening shops and offices in Harbour Town, for professional men seeking Sea Pines clients. As the whole of Sea Pines Plantation was a venture into the development of a residential and resort community, Harbour Town is a venture into commerce.

Because shelter is a basic human need, a home and a way of life are generally the largest and most important purchases a consumer makes. Sea Pines provides an unusual instance of successful marketing to a primary need in a carefully defined segment of the home-building and resort market. Together with basic planning, financing, and construction, marketing brought about the realization of one man's dream.

The marketing came first, after the land purchase. Careful marketing research and analysis were put to work before one shovelful of white Hilton Head sand was turned, one alligator disturbed, or one Hilton Head raccoon frightened into the brush. Marketing has been a basic force in bringing into being, quickly and profitably, an entire, widespread Atlantic island complex of fine homes in a pleasant setting where less than fifteen years ago there was only wilderness. It helped fundamentally to put Sea Pines Plantation on the map—literally on the automobile maps of the major oil companies—as a prestige resort and residential entity.

— 14 —
Industrial Marketing: International Nickel

There is no longer any silver in a dime, but there is still nickel in a nickel. Chances are that it came from International Nickel, for it supplies over 80 percent of the nickel used in the United States.

A hard, silver-white metallic element, nickel is old in use. Five thousand and more years ago men used it as they found it naturally fused with other metals for making tools and weapons. The ancient Chinese used nickel in a copper alloy called *pakfong*, but until the eighteenth century, Europeans found it difficult to work. They thought it a kind of copper, with which it was often mined, but it was so hard and tough when they smelted and tried to use it that German and Swedish miners called it *Kupfernickel*, the copper demon. The "nick" in nickel is the same as the "nick" in Old Nick.

Nickel was first isolated as an individual metal by A. F. Cronstedt in 1751. After five years of testing and experimentation he found that it was a distinct metallic element with its own valuable properties. Nickel is very strong. It is malleable. It can be shaped or molded. It is ductile—that is, it can easily be hammered into thin layers or drawn into fine wire without breaking. It has a high melting point, thus resists heat. It is corrosion resistant. It withstands the damaging action of many chemicals, particularly the alkalis.

Few metal objects take greater wear than coins. Gold is soft, and too valuable anyway for common use in coins of small denomination. Silver wears away with constant use. Coins made of copper alone become smooth as butter. Engraving and dates disappear from the friction and from the oils and acids in the skin of the hands as these coins are used over the years in buying and selling—used, literally, in marketing.

This marketing provided one of the first widespread uses for nickel. During the nineteenth century, nickel began to be used extensively in coinage. It is so used increasingly. Most of the countries of the world have now ceased the minting of gold and silver and are using nickel instead. United States coins are nickel over copper. Fifty-seven denominations of nickel and nickel-alloy coins were issued for the first time by twenty-eight different countries in 1968. Among them were Canada, Sweden, Egypt, the Netherlands, Brazil, and Switzerland. The new British decimal coins contain nickel and copper. Canada's coins, from its five-cent piece to its metal dollar, are of pure nickel.

Yet necessary as money always is, nickel is of far greater value for other uses.

Its most vital use is as an alloy. A small amount of nickel added to steel gives it a strength and durability surpassing any steel or any other steel alloy. Nickel and steel alloys are widely used by the construction, armament, automotive, railway, and aircraft industries. Nickel is used as an alloy in iron and steel castings and in copper and brass products. Nickel has made possible both stainless steel and Monel Metal—a corrosion-resistant alloy of nickel, copper, iron, and manganese. Stainless steel and Monel Metal are extensively used in the manufacture of industrial equipment and machine parts. The shining dye vats in textile plants are often made of one or the other. The sink in your kitchen, your knives, forks, and spoons, the hub caps of your car may be of stainless steel. It has many, many uses.

Where strength hardness and resistance to heat or rust are important, nickel alloys provide the necessary material. Commercial aircraft contain large amounts of both stainless steel and nickel alloys. There are 11,000 pounds of nickel in the airframe and engine parts of the big Boeing 747.

Storage systems for liquefied gases require the use of nickel. Water desalination plants use it to combat the corrosive effects of salt seawater. The whole petrochemical industry depends on nickel. Nickel has been built into Swedish tankers which carry liquid methane cargoes. The electronics industry depends on nickel. It has thousands of uses. Nickel has long been used for nickel plating, which gives the plated object strength and protection as well as adding to its appearance. The world demands so much nickel for industrial purposes that it cannot get enough of it.

Perennially, nickel is in short supply, so much so that in 1969 the United States Treasury was forced to release for defense purposes 9,000,000 pounds being held for coinage. International Nickel produced 480,840,000 pounds of nickel in 1968 and planned greater production in 1969, but a 128-day strike interfered, and 1969 production dropped to 382,170,000 pounds. Early in 1970 the United States government freed an additional 20,000,000 pounds of nickel for delivery to defense industries on the agreement that International Nickel would return an equivalent amount in upgraded form in 1971 and 1972.

The International Nickel Company of Canada, Ltd., was formed in 1902 by a merging of earlier mining and refining organizations. Now a multinational company with more than 34,000 employees in eighteen different countries, it has two principal research and marketing-oriented subsidiaries: International Nickel, Ltd., in Great Britain and The International Nickel Company, Inc., in the United States.

In this country, International Nickel, which has its corporate offices in New York, has rolling mills in West Virginia, research laboratories in Sterling Forest, New York, and on Harbor Island off the coast of North Carolina, and other properties and facilities. It has refineries in Acton, just outside London; plants in

Hereford, England; and refineries in Clydach, Wales. But its principal installations—those on which all of the others depend —are in two parts of Canada.

In the Sudbury District of the Province of Ontario, where nickel-producing ore has been mined since 1886, International Nickel has the world's largest nickel-producing complex. Over a wide expanse, but all within a thirty-mile radius of Copper Cliff, it has mines, mills, smelters, and refineries, all connected by rail. The company has a somewhat smaller but also major installation in Thompson, Manitoba. In fact, it created Thompson. After years of exploration, at a cost of $10 million, to locate the ore and make sure that the deposit could be commercially mined, it not only opened the mines and built the mining and refining complex, but also built the roads, houses, schools, and the community facilities that, physically, are the town. In one decade, between 1957 and 1967, International Nickel built the third-largest community in Manitoba at a total cost of over $200 million.

Like oil, nickel lies deep in the bowels of the earth, where it has lain for geologic ages. It takes geologists to find it, miners and mining engineers to get the ore to the surface, smelters to extract the metal from the ore, metallurgists and other scientific workers to test it for new and old uses—and marketers to get nickel to the hundreds of industries which put it to thousands of uses.

The primary product of International Nickel emerges for the market in several forms: as cathodes, and pellets or shot for the melting furnaces in the making of steel alloys; as nickel-oxide sinter packed in steel cans for direct charging into various types of furnaces producing nickel-alloy steels; as nickel powder for powder metallurgy; as oxides and salts of nickel for the chemical industries.

International Nickel also produces copper (208,220,000 pounds of it in 1969), a major element in its ores, and iron, sulfur, and cobalt, and other elements—fifteen in all. As by-products (but what by-products!) it produces gold, silver, and the platinum-group precious metals. These are extracted from the residue accumulated in the electrolytic tanks in its nickel and copper refineries. The current price of electrolytic nickel in the United States is $1.28 a pound; the price of platinum is $132.50 an ounce, troy weight. In 1969, International Nickel delivered 421,500 ounces of gold and the platinum-group metals and 1,111,000 ounces of silver.

International Nickel makes no consumer products, yet there is nickel in something you use every day, probably in several somethings. Sometimes it is visible; sometimes it is not. Your clock or your watch may have nickel or nickel-plated parts in it. Your barometer or other instruments, faucets, lamps, hardware fixtures, exposed plumbing, bathroom fixtures, and electric-light wall-switch plates may well be nickel-plated for both decorative and wear-resistant purposes. There is nickel in the chrome-and-steel bumpers of automobiles, in the rims and setting of headlights, and in functioning parts of automobile frames and engines. Your flashlight, transistor radio, or tape recorder may work on cadmium nickel batteries. There may be nickel in the gears as well as in the handlebars and other shining parts of your bicycle. You may have German silver in jewelry, coins, or decorative metal on various objects. German silver, an alloy of nickel, zinc, and copper, which is sometimes called nickel silver, is also used in making cutlery and as a base in plating.

To get this metal, International Nickel is continually prospecting all over the world for new and workable ore deposits, but the search is not done by the traditional bearded prospector and his laden burro.

International Nickel's prospectors fly about a million miles every year, using electromagnetic equipment to probe hundreds of feet below the earth's surface. A continuous film records the location of the aircraft and coordinates it with the readings on their ore-locating instruments. As in warfare, the infantry follows the air force. Field parties track down sites which show possible ore deposits. Drilling for samples follows. International Nickel spent very nearly twenty million dollars in this kind of world-wide prospecting in 1969. This was a record, but every year it spends in the millions of dollars exploring for new nickel-yielding ores.

It is drilling near Ely, Minnesota, and evaluating ore dis-coveries there. It is investigating nickel deposits in Indonesia and in western Australia. One of the largest known deposits of nickel is on the French Pacific island of New Caledonia. Under agreement with the French government and a group of public and private French interests, International Nickel is exploring development of untapped sources of nickel there.

The company is prospecting in other parts of Canada, in Africa, Panama, Costa Rica, Guatemala, and in the states of Washington, Arizona, and Virginia. It is continuing its investi-gations of the sea as a possible nickel source. Testing and ex-perimentation to find out whether sites discovered can be economically mined on a commercial scale often takes years of work and large expenditures before the new deposits prove out—or do not.

The marketing of an industrial product, especially a vital material like nickel, is very different from the consumer market-ing of a beverage, foodstuffs, office equipment, or resort home. Nickel goes to a well-defined market in many nickel-using in-dustries. It is purchased for these industries by engineers and production men. They buy nickel only because they need it for industrial use in the manufacture of machinery and equipment or of consumer or consumer-used end products. They buy it because it is the best, usually the only, material that will meet their requirements; and they buy it because they expect—at least plan—to make a profit through marketing the products in which they use it.

These industrial customers are not swayed by emotion, as individuals so often are in their buying. Thus there is no mass, class, or selective marketing here. There is no impulse buying.

The men who buy nickel for business purposes are not apt to be susceptible to glamorous advertising.

Nickel is sold directly to its industrial users, and the men who sell it must know its uses in the special fields in which they market. These men, whom International Nickel calls its "application engineers," to distinguish them from engineers engaged in production, really act many times as consultants to nickel-using industrial customers. They must understand forging and foundry work, steel making, battery making, automotive and aircraft manufacturing, or whatever their specialties. They must know the problems companies in these industries face and be able to help solve them where nickel is concerned; and to point out where the use of nickel or of more nickel will enable the buyer to make a better product at a greater profit.

The overall objective of International Nickel's marketing is to widen the market for nickel by creating new industrial uses for it and by promoting nickel-containing products made by its customers. Personal selling has to play the larger part in industrial marketing of this kind, yet industrial marketers do use advertising, and International Nickel advertises for carefully planned reasons.

Over the years manufacturers or producers of so-called hidden products who market nothing to the general public have advertised to make their companies widely and favorably known, to acquaint people with their contribution to the consumer products made by others, and to support their industrial customers with advertising which assures the public that the end products it buys contain good parts or materials.

Botany Mills advertises its woolens, Minneapolis-Honeywell its automatic devices, E. I. du Pont de Nemours its synthetic fibers, United States Steel its steel, ALCOA its aluminum. Chemical producers like Monsanto, Union Carbide, and American Cyanamid, and others like Armco Steel Corporation (American Rolling Mills Company) and the Timken Roller Bearing Company have all advertised in mass-circulation consumer media.

International Nickel prepares and publishes technical data, studies, and handbooks, which it distributes to actual and potential users of nickel. It advertises to the trade, to well-informed readers who know nickel and its uses. In 1955 it deliberately went into a mass advertising medium to augment this marketing effort, and it has remained in it. It entered radio.

The company uses spot announcements in the top-rated news programs in various city markets. It chose this method of reaching the general public because these news programs have a large audience of men, many of them in industry. The programs, of course, are current. They are up to the hour or the minute, and they are factual; so is the International Nickel advertising. As sound advertising usually is, it is quiet and restrained. What it talks about is the importance of nickel to everyone because of the part that the metal plays in industry. It tells what nickel is, of the strength it gives to nickel-alloy steels, and of how it is used, for instance, in the construction of aircraft or in underwater investigation. The advertising stresses International Nickel's technological contributions to industry and the company's continuous research.

A typical program comes on the air at about seven thirty A.M. in this way: "Here is the WTIC [Hartford, Connecticut] news brought to you today by International Nickel, where imaginative research in metals is the basis for tomorrow's products." The news of wars, riots, and more personalized crimes with a sprinkling of strikes and local disasters follows. Then comes one in the continuing series of International Nickel's carefully informed messages which carries its own interest. It could be this one:

> It was Aristotle in the fourth century B.C. who told us that all matter consisted of only four elements: air, water, earth and fire, in varying proportions, with only four properties: hot, cold, wet, and dry. So awesome was Aristotle that more than twenty centuries passed before we dared to question. For this we may thank Lavoisier, the

father of chemistry, who stated with logic and evidence that an element was any matter that could not be further decomposed, listed more than thirty, and declared further that, depending on temperature, an element could be a gas, a liquid, or a solid. In the two centuries since, the elements have grown to over one hundred. The twenty-eighth element is nickel—hard, white, tough, durable—aiding technology in aerospace, medicine, electronics, oceanology, and other vital fields. As knowledge multiplies, so does the need for nickel, and so do the research efforts of the people of International Nickel.

International Nickel uses its print and electronic advertising to make people aware of its corporate identity. It assures the public as well as its industrial customers that, in the face of a continuing shortage, it is doing all it can to supply their needs. Its advertising expresses confidence in nickel's place in the future as International Nickel continues to produce a necessity for many products that fulfill human needs. It supports the company's industrial customers by telling the public over the air of the qualities and values of nickel.

The company's print advertising reaches industrial customers and prospective customers in their professional capacities. Its radio advertising reaches some of these men, too, but also others who are not directly concerned. As one executive of The International Nickel Company, Inc., phrases it, "People don't know who we are and relatively few know what nickel is, what it's used for, or how important it is in their lives." International Nickel uses carefully selected radio outlets to tell them.

Its advertising has one other important purpose. It keeps International Nickel's name and standing as well as knowledge of its contribution to economic and technological advance in the consciousness of actual and potential investors. Like other large companies, International Nickel must continually borrow from banks, other financial institutions, and individuals seeking to commit capital in the expectation of making a profit. This money is needed for expansion, for exploration, for scientific and marketing research, and for all of the other activities that must be performed to ensure the maintenance and continued growth of an important organization in an important industry.

Marketing is as vital in basic industry as in the manufacture and distribution of consumer goods and products. A fundamental part of the marketing effort is direct personal selling to industry, often, as in this instance, to many industries. This selling is supported by factual announcements to the trade. Personal selling and trade announcements are then supplemented by consumer advertising which jumps the intervening operations by communicating directly with the consuming public.

— 15 —

Restrictions on Marketing

Marketing in the United States operates under many governmental restrictions. Some laws are intended to enforce competition among manufacturers and distributors and to prevent any one of them from obtaining a monopoly of the market for its product. Some are intended to protect the small wholesaler and retailer from competition by the large quantity buyer. Still others are meant for the protection of the consumer. The government also exerts strong controls on marketing through heavy taxation, which gives it virtual control of both large corporations and small enterprises.

The Sherman Antitrust Act was passed in 1890 to check the abuses of predatory corporations which were then annihilating competition by legal but hardly ethical means. Through the economies effected by mass production and large-scale buying at heavy discounts, they could undersell smaller competitors. They could move into a market, sell below cost, take the loss in one place, and make it up in another. In this way they could force other companies out of business or could take them over at their own price. Public agitations against the trusts, as the large corporate combines were called, resulted. The purpose of the Sherman Antitrust Act is to prevent unfair competition of this kind and prevent the monopoly of a market which enables the company controlling it to set any prices it chooses and to do business arbitrarily under its own terms.

The provisions of this law were left vague so that it could be interpreted to fit any given case against a company and its officers. The law made violation a criminal offense, providing fines and imprisonment on conviction. Corporations have been heavily fined and their executives jailed in successful government prosecutions. Other corporations have been forced to dissolve or to break into smaller units.

In 1914 the Clayton Antitrust Act was passed to strengthen previous legislation. Again monopoly was forbidden. A manufacturer had to sell, without price discrimination, on the same terms to all buyers. He could not require buyers not to handle the products of competitors. Corporations were forbidden to acquire stock in another company if this acted to lessen competition.

In the same year, the Federal Trade Commission was established. It was charged with investigating the activities of any persons or companies suspected of antitrust violations. The act establishing the commission once more forbade all unfair competition. The FTC sets up trade regulations in meetings with industry, and its rulings have the effect of law as the commission can apply for federal court action against those it indicts as offenders.

The Clayton Act was expanded in 1936 by the Robinson-Patman Act. This law forbade all kinds of kickbacks, advertising allowances, and the like. Discounts to quantity buyers were allowed, but a manufacturer could allow no special concessions to any dealer. There could be no price-fixing by agreement of competing companies under any of these laws.

Interpretation of these measures is difficult for lawyers, jurists, and trade officials as well as for manufacturers and marketers. This makes their equitable application difficult in any given instance. Many cases have been under continual or periodic FTC investigation and in and out of the courts for years. Sometimes the FTC seems inquisitorial in pressing its charges; at other times it seems satisfied if the illusion of competition is maintained. Some industries are by nature monopolistic; no other organization has the facilities, the finances, the skills or the market to produce and distribute whatever the product is.

In 1963 a Supreme Court justice (quoted by Harold M. Fleming in *Gasoline Prices and Competition,* 1966) called the Robinson-Patman Act "a singularly opaque and elusive statute."

By law, prices may not be fixed at the manufacturing level, but government is no more consistent than any other body. It has passed laws that, instead of forbidding it, uphold price-fixing at the retail level. California passed the first Fair Trade Act in 1931. This permitted manufacturers to sign agreements with dealers setting specific prices on retail items no matter in what store sold. By an extension of the law in 1933, one agreement between one manufacturer and one retailer made the price mandatory on all retailers in the state. Every retailer who stocked the lawn mower, proprietary medicine, toothpaste, or whatever it was had to charge the same stipulated price. All but three of the then forty-eight states passed similar laws. A federal law, the Miller-Tydings Act, was passed in 1937, making fair-trade prices mandatory in interstate commerce. The McGuire Act of 1952 made nonsigners as well as signers to fair-trade agreements liable.

The fair-trade laws never worked well. Less than 10 percent of nationally branded merchandise was thus price-fixed. Manufacturers did not have to extend such agreements. If they did, competing marketers could undercut the fair-trade prices by differently branded or unbranded merchandise of equal or superior quality. Fair-trade price-fixing has been abandoned in many of the states where it was once written into law.

After a long and hard-hitting crusade campaign by several consumer magazines, notably *Collier's* and *Ladies' Home Journal,* the federal government passed the Food and Drug Act of 1906. This law required a label on containers of foods and drugs listing their ingredients and giving the name of the manufacturers responsible for the products. This law for the protection of the consumer was expanded by the federal Food, Drug, and Cosmetic Act of 1938, which extended its provisions. By another law of 1962, all new drugs must have the approval of the Food and Drug Administration before they can be marketed.

Labeling for the protection of the buyer and user is mandatory under additional federal statutes. The Wool Products Labeling Act of 1939, the Fur Products Act of 1951, and the Textile Fiber Products Identification Act of 1958 are all enforced by the Federal Trade Commission. The Hazardous Substances Labeling Act of 1960 is enforced by the Department of Health, Education, and Welfare. The Automobile Information Disclosure Act of 1958 forces automobile dealers to display window stickers on all new cars showing the factory-suggested price of the car and the cost to the purchaser of all options and accessories.

Other laws which affect marketing protect the consumer in other ways. False and misleading advertising is prohibited under state laws. It is also forbidden under provisions of the Federal Trade Act and, of course, is subject to prosecution under all the legal safeguards against fraud.

Through a maze of laws and revisions of laws and amendments to laws enacted since the 1930's and administered by the United States Department of Agriculture, the federal government directly affects the marketing of many farm products and the prices paid for them by consumers. The government underwrites farm markets by establishing parity, that is, fair or equal prices on basic agricultural commodities such as wheat, corn, barley, rice, cotton, tobacco, sorghum, and, at various times, other products. It then maintains these markets in two ways.

To guard against overproduction which would glut the market and lower prices to the farmer, the federal government limits production by reducing the land acreage used to raise specific crops. Farmers are paid not to raise them. They allow their land to lie fallow or put it into grass and trees to prevent erosion—place their land in "soil banks" or practice approved methods of soil conservation. They are then paid, every year, amounts of money equivalent to that which they might have made had they used the land productively.

At the other end of the process, through a complicated system of loans, the government purchases surplus farm commodities and puts them into storage or into what it sometimes calls strategic stockpiles. Tremendous amounts of food, billions of dollars' worth, are thus kept in storage and off the market in order to keep up consumer prices.

Some of the stored foods are disbursed in many ways, all of them duly prescribed by law. Under the Agricultural, Trade Development and Assistance Act of 1954 as Amended (Public Law 480), surplus agricultural commodities may be sold by the United States to obtain foreign currency, to procure military or strategic equipment abroad, or to pay national obligations to other countries. The money thus obtained is generally lent back to the countries from which it comes. Government surplus food may be sold to finance international educational exchange activities, to pay for the translation, publication, and distribution of books and periodicals (including government publications) abroad, and for a long list of other approved purposes.

Public Law 480 also makes it possible to make surplus foods available for famine relief and kindred assistance to friendly countries, and "to assist friendly nations to be independent of trade with the Union of Soviet Socialist Republics and with nations dominated or controlled by the Union of Soviet Socialist Republics. . . ."

Surplus farm commodities may be used, too, for food-stamp programs and similar welfare relief purposes.

Despite these uses, the amounts of surplus food in government storage remain huge. Just storing them is intricate and expensive big business. Yet this is certainly preferable to dumping coffee or destroying other commodities in order to achieve the scarcity which ensures high prices and high profits.

During the Depression of 1933, when people desperately needed both food and clothing, the federal government plowed up ten million acres of cotton and killed six million pigs that were not yet marketable. This was to maintain prices for the farmer, for there was then a surplus of hogs and corn. Prices were low and would get lower by the time these pigs would have been ready for slaughter. They were turned over to the Department of Agriculture at processing and packing plants, the farmers were paid, and the pork was distributed to families on relief. The price of pork rose steeply in 1935 when, due to a drought, there was short supply of feed corn.

The mechanics of the procedure change in detail under successive administrations and the actions taken by different Congresses, but billions of dollars are spent annually in federal farm subsidies. Tremendous sums go into handling, storing, and financing of the surplus foods. A high percentage of United States farm income is derived from this government source.

These farm-price supports have often been attacked as discriminatory because they favor one segment of the economy over other segments and the few at the expense of the many. Not only do they constitute huge direct expenditure of taxpayer funds, but they also increase food prices to the general consumer. Government cold storage of butter, for instance, is largely responsible for its high price in the supermarket and other grocery outlets.

Taxes of many kinds levied at various stages of the manufacturing and marketing process by federal, state, and local governments—primarily by the federal government—strongly affect marketing and add appreciably to consumer prices. Giant General Foods has about 42,000 employees around the world. The Internal Revenue Service, tax-collecting agency of the federal government, has 60,000 employees in Washington, seven regional offices, fifty-eight district offices, and about nine hundred local offices. A few years ago someone counted the hidden taxes in one loaf of bread. They came to well over a hundred. Almost everything the consumer buys and uses is taxed, often several times by several different agencies and by the same agencies as it changes hands before it reaches him.

Just as the federal government takes anywhere from one quarter or one third on up of the income of every individual, it takes the largest share of the profits of successful marketing. Every year a corporation of any size must generally pay taxes amounting to more than it can pay its owners—its shareholders—as dividends or retain for expansion and improvement of its business.

The Coca-Cola Company showed a gross profit of $251,041,702 in 1969. Out of this amount, taxes on income came to $130,022,000. The 1969 income before taxes of the Xerox Corporation was $389,722,000; income taxes took $204,500,000 of this profit. Before federal income taxes, the income of Federated Department Stores, Inc., in 1969 was $169,941,543. After taxes, currently payable and deferred, that income had been reduced to $84,000,000.

The country's largest corporation, General Motors, had gross sales for all its products of $24,295,141,000 in 1969. Out of this gross, GM's net income was $1,710,695,000. In United States and foreign income taxes, state and local taxes, and the corporation's share of Social Security taxes, General Motors paid out $2,536,700,000—or more than twice its total net income. GM shareholders, of course, paid their individual income taxes on their dividends which had already been taxed at their source; and GM employees paid income and other taxes on their salaries or wages.

The automobile is an everyday necessity in American life, used for going to and from work, school, or shopping. Yet the automobile is still taxed—its manufacture, its marketing, its purchase, and its use—as if it were the "gasoline pleasure car" of 1910. In 1968, the last year for which figures are available, the federal excise tax on new cars was $1.531 billion, and the excise tax on trucks and buses came to another $448 million. The federal excise tax on gasoline motor fuel came to $3.931 billion. There were additional federal taxes, of course, on tires, lubricating oils, and automotive accessories.

All of these taxes must be absorbed in the cost of the vehicles marketed to purchasers. A substantial part of the price of any new car is in the hidden federal taxes which the buyer must pay. He must then pay any state and local sales, excise, and use taxes, and continue to pay both federal and state taxes, possibly municipal taxes as well, as long as he uses the car.

In Massachusetts, for instance, the new car buyer must pay a sales tax of 3 percent on the purchase price of a new car. As in other states, he will pay registration and driver's license fees. Personal and property-damage liability insurance is compulsory in the commonwealth, and the rates are high. In addition, the Massachusetts new car buyer must pay a state excise tax of $66 on 90 percent of each $1000 of the manufacturer's list price of the car the first year; the same amount on 60 percent the second; on 40 percent the third; and on down to 10 percent after the fifth year. This excise tax never goes lower than that.

Massachusetts charges tolls on its major highways, and the Massachusetts tax on gasoline is currently seven cents a gallon. As the federal tax on the same gallon of gasoline is four cents, this means that the motorist pays eleven cents, or more than a quarter of the retail price, in taxes.

According to the American Petroleum Institute, when all of the taxes placed against a gallon of gasoline are considered— those which the industry pays as well as those the motorist pays directly—taxes account for about one half of the price to the consumer of a gallon of gasoline. Gasoline itself sold for 22.11 cents a gallon in 1957 and for 24.38 cents in April, 1969, but taxes have increased twice as fast as the consumer price of the product. In 1967 the net income of the petroleum industry from operations in the United States was about $4.9 billion. Direct operating taxes came to $2.5 billion or more than half this income.

Taxes of these and other kinds restrict marketing in several ways. They limit the distributive efforts of the manufacturer by curtailing his profits. They raise the prices of goods and services all down the line. They mitigate against consumer buying when taxes make prices prohibitive. Through the personal income tax—and this is deliberate policy—government limits the amounts of money the consumer can keep and spend, or what is called "disposable personal income."

The dollar which has already been heavily taxed will be taxed again when it is spent, and it has already been so enfeebled by inflation that its strength has about gone. The dollar is not inflated. It is deflated. It is prices that are inflated, and the ability of the dollar to cope with them diminishes daily.

According to the Bureau of Labor Statistics of the United States Department of Labor, the dollar—considered to be at par value 1957–1959—was worth $2.05 in terms of consumer prices in 1940. In 1968, the dollar was worth 82.5 cents. That is, the dollar has depreciated by about 125 percent. This is fantastic arithmetic, but it is a grim fact.

Government sources show that a dozen eggs which cost 33 cents in 1940 cost over 60 cents in 1969. Apples went from 5.5 cents a pound to more than 24; round steak from about 36.5 cents a pound to $1.19 a pound; bacon from a little over 27 cents to 81 cents, and a can of peas from 13.5 cents to 24.5 cents. A check in any market will show higher prices now than government statisticians used. Sliced bacon, at the moment, is nearer $1.20 a pound, and the other items are correspondingly more expensive.

What was the 10- or 15-cent ice cream soda is 65 cents or more at the fountain. The 5-cent cup of coffee is 15 or 20 cents in the cheaper restaurants. The 5- or 10-cent magazine is now 50 or 75 cents. The price of first-class postage more than doubled at the same time that mail delivery service was cut in half. The penny newspaper is at least a dime. Penny candy is a dime. Grossly inflated prices have become commonplace.

The automobile which sold for about $800 when the United States entered World War Two is now sold anywhere from perhaps $3,200 to nearly $5,000. It is larger. It goes faster, and it has more shiny things on it, but generally it is less durable. It simply takes you from hither to yon and—if you are lucky—back again, just as the older car did.

One chief cause of inflation is the swollen and swelling costs of government, with its millions of employees and its uninhibited spending for wars and countless welfare programs. Another major cause is the multiplied cost of unionized labor. Labor's demands, enforced by paralyzing strikes, keep adding to the cost of both production and marketing; and all of these costs are passed on to the helpless consumer. The butcher, the baker, and the candlestick maker keep trying to outdo each other in arbitrary demands for higher wages and more benefits. They always get them because industry-wide strikes in one industry affect many other industries and make life unpleasant for large parts of the population, and because politicians, no matter what the administration, need the support of organized labor and its votes.

As these two major causes flourish abundantly, inflation can only continue. Even for the victorious who gain the spoils, the ratio of earnings to the capacity to buy does not change appreciably. It makes little real difference whether a man or woman is paid twenty-five cents an hour and a loaf of bread costs five cents, or whether the worker is paid five dollars an hour and the same loaf, or one not as appetizing or nutritious, costs one dollar. It makes a great deal of difference, of course, to those who do not get the increased wages but still must pay the higher prices.

One other cause contributing to inflation is psychological rather than economic. Whether it is earned or comes from welfare sources, more people have more money to spend. They like to spend it, and they like showing that they have it to spend. There is something splendid about carefree extravagance. People enjoy leaving as a restaurant tip what a few years ago would have been the price of the entire meal. The allowance of a child is often what was his grandfather's weekly wage, and he has only to ask for more. It's only money, and the union or an obedient Congress will get you more next year.

It is this attitude which government righteously singles out as the villain in the piece. Thus it cites taxation as a means of controlling inflation. What people do not have they cannot spend; thus it is only a kindness to take it away from them. Then government can spend more and more of the dollars that wilt away.

Marketing is restricted, sometimes constricted, by laws, regulatory government bodies, taxation, and inflation. Yet, as it has always been, it is most affected by what people will buy, how much they will buy, how often they will buy, where they will buy, what prices they will pay, and how well or how poorly marketed products meet their actual or emotional requirements.

— 16 —

Consumer Education

There are and have been for a long time many organizations devoted to consumer education and protection. These include federal and state governmental bodies, university departments in home economics and allied subjects, and private groups organized into various associations. There are also individuals who act professionally as zealous consumer defenders and advisers.

People have been conscious of themselves as buyers and users of many products for almost as long as there have been markets offering objects for their pleasure or discomfiture. As already pointed out, women are often the shoppers for themselves and for their families. Through necessity, long experience, their love of a bargain, and their natural wish to obtain the most for their money, they are deeply concerned with marketing at the buying end.

The women's magazines were shrewd enough to perceive this early. Well before the turn of the twentieth century, *Ladies' Home Journal* guaranteed its readers against loss if products purchased through advertising in its pages were found to be below stated standards. Soon afterward its publisher, Cyrus H. K. Curtis, banned all patent-medicine advertising, all advertising for cosmetics, and all financial advertising from the magazine.

Ladies' Home Journal did its best to protect its readers against possible fraud. It would accept only honest advertising for sound products. Though other highly respected general magazines accepted patent-medicine and other kinds of questionable advertising, the magazine did this to safeguard its consumer-readers and also to protect itself. The repute of *Ladies' Home Journal* and the faith women had in it depended upon their satisfactory experience with its advertising as well as with its articles and stories.

Before long, *Ladies' Home Journal* went much farther. At a time when patent medicines were insistently advertised and widely used, the magazine attacked them in a fierce crusade. It showed that some nostrums were actually poisonous, others injurious, and many more completely worthless. *Collier's,* which had many women readers, allied itself with its competitor, and the two magazines were strongly instrumental in forcing passage of the first pure food and drug legislation.

Other magazines written for women readers joined in the fight to aid and protect the consumer. The once very influential but now extinct *Woman's Home Companion,* under its strong editor, Gertrude Battles Lane, crusaded against "the cat in the cracker barrel" and helped bring about the sanitary packaging of groceries. *Good Housekeeping* inaugurated its Good House-keeping Institute in 1901, and it developed laboratories and kitchens to test household appliances, textiles, cleaning agents, and the like. Later, with Dr. H. W. Wiley, who as chief chemist of the Department of Agriculture had fought for the pure food laws, it founded its Good Housekeeping Bureau. It investigated food products, drugs, and cosmetics, and published the results for all to read. The Good Housekeeping Seal of Approval has long been known and accepted.

Other magazines did comparable consumer education and protection work, and one popular general monthly, *McClure's,* which is no longer published, went all out for it in the first decade of the twentieth century. *McClure's* hired a group of brilliant reporters and writers—Ida Tarbell, Ray Stannard Baker, and Lincoln Steffens among them—and published the articles of other comparable writers. They became known as the "muckrakers." What they did was investigate large corporations, city governments, finance, life insurance, the Senate, railroads, meatpackers, and other private or public activities. Then they exposed the evils they uncovered in sensational but well-documented articles which aroused great public interest and indignation and led in some instances to sweeping reforms.

The muckrakers found nothing to praise and much to condemn. Their intent was not to protect the consumer but to sell magazines and books, but the effect of their startling reports was such that often consumer protection resulted. A number of industries were forced by law or strong public opinion to mend their ways.

A crusading novelist and journalist, Upton Sinclair, provoked other reforms through his sensational exposures. A prolific writer who burned with indignation at injustice, Sinclair was commissioned by a socialist magazine to write a novel about the unsavory conditions under which many packinghouse people worked. *The Jungle,* published in 1906, was the result. It headlined the economic and social injustices and the evidences of political corruption in the packing industry, but, more than that, described vividly the foul conditions under which some meats were produced. Readers were horrified, and they were consumers every one. *The Jungle* helped provoke imposition of sanitary standards which benefited the consumer.

Like some of the widely publicized consumer actions of the 1960's, these activities of the muckrakers were deliberate onslaughts on suspect industries or companies. They were meant to be attacks, exposés of evils and inadequacies, and to foment improvement. There have been many such attempts, some of them effective for the consumer in results obtained, but the strong body of organized consumer education and protection came into being in the 1930's, and has continued steadily and quietly or noisily ever since.

The consumer movement was born of the Depression. Of necessity people needed to know how best to spend their money —when they had any—and for what. They needed honest information on values. They were less interested in exposures of misdeeds in production and distribution than in knowing what products and what brands of those products were good, bad, or indifferent. People wanted realistic appraisal and usable practical advice.

Again sensationalism came first. *Your Money's Worth* by Stuart Chase and F. J. Schlink, an all-out attack on false advertising, was published in 1927. The next year Chase and Schlink formed the Consumer's Club, its avowed purpose to protect the consumer against predators. In 1929 this club became Consumers' Research, Inc. in Washington, New Jersey, with Schlink as president. Schlink and the group around him quickly exploited the market for sensational exposure.

In 1933 came *100,000,000 Guinea Pigs* by F. J. Schlink and Arthur Kallet, secretary of Consumers' Research. An exposé of food and drug advertising, this book was a best seller. It appeared during the darkest time of the Depression, with the public anxious to find a villain for all its miseries, and advertising was a convenient choice. Many of the lurid revelations in the book were outdated examples from trials and investigations into cases of fraud and misrepresentation. They were far from being representative of advertising and marketing as a whole. The formula established, more such books by the same or associated authors came quickly: *Skin Deep,* by M. C. Phillips (who was Mrs. F. J. Schlink) in 1934; *Eat, Drink, and Be Wary,* by F. J. Schlink in 1935; *Partners in Plunder,* by J. B. Matthews, a Consumers' Research vice president, and R. E. Shallcross, in 1935. These books did not gain the attention of *100,000,000 Guinea Pigs.* The vein had been worked out, and Consumers' Research settled to its business as a product-testing organization.

It examined advertised brands of products, then published bulletins stating whether or not they lived up to the claims made for them. These and an annual cumulative bulletin labeled articles as "Recommended," "Intermediate," or "Not Recommended." The bulletins were mailed to subscribers for their private use, and these subscribers were urged to send in newspaper and magazine clippings or circulars which might lead to uncovering more evils in advertising. Ironically, Consumers' Research, which condemned advertising in toto, used all it could get and use in any way possible.

Consumers' Research was struck by some of the evils it deplored. Officers of the organization refused to recognize a union of its office workers. The workers went out on strike, claiming that they were underpaid and that the heads of Consumers' Research, which advertised itself as nonprofit, were overpaid. The organization refused to arbitrate and demanded and got police protection from its erstwhile employees and associates.

As a result, the strikers withdrew and formed a competing consumers' group, Consumers' Union, in New York. The college professor and economist Colston E. Warne became its president. Immediately, Consumers' Union took a full-page advertisement in *The New Republic* to explain its case and state its purposes.

Consumers' Union, which promoted itself as its subscribers' Bureau of Standards (after the National Bureau of Standards of the United States Department of Commerce), set up a testing process like that of its parent company and bitter rival. Like the original organization, it issued reports of its findings, but classified advertised brands of various products—automobiles, shoes, appliances, etc.—as "Best Buy," "Also Acceptable," and "Not Acceptable." It began issuance of its *Consumers' Union Buying Guide,* which it described as "a far better guide to intelligent purchasing than any other ordinarily available to the consumer." The Union advertised widely and, like the commercially published magazines, urged its subscribers to give gift subscriptions to their friends.

Consumers' Union reports did not always criticize adversely. It found good in many advertised products and said so; it found bad in others and said that too. Its "Best Buy" became an accolade marketers were happy to obtain.

Consumer education continues as an established activity through such organizations, through governmental advice, through testing laboratories set up by independent bodies and dissemination of the facts they find and the opinions they reach. Whether all such testing is adequate has often been questioned. It can seldom match in extent and thoroughness the testing that manufacturers themselves conduct or the research and experimenting put into product improvement.

Any manufacturer and distributor is always suspect. The company is in business to make money. Perhaps that is also its highest recommendation. The producer and distributor cannot make money on a large scale in the national or international market over a period of time unless the customer receives what he considers to be his money's worth. Consumer satisfaction is the best guarantee of continued success, and hard competition with other marketers in the same field is a sharp spur toward trying to gain and keep the customer approval without which no maker or seller can stay in business very long.

Because the subject is naturally one of wide interest, popular magazines like *The Reader's Digest* run informative articles on what to look for and check in the purchase of a new or used car, how to guard against being overcharged for automobile or watch repairs, and other articles which state by brand name which cigarettes contain the most or the least tars and nicotine. Special interest magazines scrutinize marketed articles within their fields of interest. Automotive periodicals, for instance, pick a make and model which they present as the best of a season, thus indirectly recommend for purchase.

Occasionally an onslaught after the old muckraking manner produces results still, drawing attention to the subject discussed as well as publicity for the attack and attacker. Ralph Nader's outcry *Unsafe at Any Speed,* targeted at the automotive industry, helped bring about the incorporation of additional safety features in the manufacture of automobiles. These have been made obligatory by law. Other consumer advocates have attacked advertised dry cereals as lacking nutriment, but thus far provoked only indignant denials from their processors.

The sensible buyer has always used caution in making his purchases and observed the old adage *caveat emptor,* "let the buyer beware." The consumer has his own experience and common sense to guide him, but he can generally use all the help he can get. The consumer movement has provided some useful aids and also acts as a deterrent to the overblown claims made by some marketers and as an incentive to the production and distribution of dependable merchandise.

— 17 —

Marketing Research: Conclusion

Suppose a processor of tobacco products has or buys an idea for a new kind of chewing tobacco which he can market in anise, clove, and allspice flavors. He knows where he can obtain an ample supply of good Kentucky black Burley at below-market price. He has methods of curing and treating it in his plant, and he can have a package designed that will have an irresistible appeal to tobacco chewers. Physically and financially, he is equipped to produce the new product, but first he must know whether or not he can sell such a chewing tobacco profitably.

He conducts a market inquiry or he hires an organization whose business it is to do this marketing research for him. Millions on millions of dollars are spent every year in marketing research of this kind. Studies are made and surveys conducted by manufacturers, by large retailers, by advertising agencies who must be able to advise their clients, and by the advertising media.

Marketing-research reports are often voluminous compilations of graphs and charts, together with more pages of solemn statistics, and then more pages analyzing them. The reports look complicated and mysterious, and often they are purposely made to look so. In essence, marketing research is very simple. It is

173

done just by asking people questions and recording their answers. The researchers do not ask everyone, but they ask a representative sample of the population of the country, of a geographical region, or of a city, or of some particular professional or social group whose answers are needed. The census is taken in this way. Public-opinion polls (pollsters adopted the technique from marketing research) are taken in this way. In large manufacturing plants not every item is inspected, but every tenth car—or whatever number—that comes off the assembly line, every twenty-fifth package of cereal, or every one-hundredth can of peas.

Marketing research for the proposed new chewing tobacco would select a mathematically accurate sample—generally what is known as an "area probability sample"—and then, either through personal interview, by mail, or by telephone, ask that group of people questions like these: Do you chew tobacco? If you do, how many packages a day do you chew? What is your favorite flavor? Do you chew more at work or more at home? What brand do you usually purchase? Do you buy it yourself or does your wife (husband, please check one) buy it for you? Do you chew more between the hours of six and nine A.M. or between six and twelve P.M.?

Besides questions like these, respondents would be asked questions of another kind. Age? Male or female? Married or single? Elementary-school graduate? High school? College? How many are in your family? What is the vocation of the family head? Do you own your own home? What is your annual family income? Answers to these questions give the inquirer the social or demographic characteristics of the market.

When the field work has been completed, the answers obtained are tabulated. That is, the marketing-research department or organization counts up the yes, no, and don't-know answers. Counts are made of the answers to every question and the results cross-tabulated. Results of this tabulation tell the tobacco processor much that he needs to know. He discovers that his primary market is in the North, the South, or elsewhere. He can gauge how much of his potential market lies in rural places and small towns and how much in cities of 100,000-and-over population. He finds that his market is chiefly among men rather than women, or the reverse; in families whose annual income is from $5000 to $10,000, or perhaps in those with family incomes above $50,000 a year. He may find out that most of his customers will be between five and fifteen years of age, but more likely that they will be between eighteen and eighty. From the results of his marketing research, the tobacco processor has some idea how many packages of his new chewing tobacco he can expect to sell the first year and which flavor he had better concentrate on producing.

Some of it on a very large scale and costing huge amounts of money, marketing research of this kind is conducted for branded grocery products, meats, television sets, toothpastes, detergents, and many, many other products. The research is done not just once but usually on a continuing basis, for people and marketing conditions change.

Long before he starts production on next year's line, the automotive manufacturer knows what colors people prefer and whether the man or the woman in a family makes the final purchase decision. The maker and marketer of table flatware knows what styles and prices of table flatware brides prefer this year, what older women will buy as replacements, and what grandmothers favor as presents for their grandchildren. A manufacturer of dish towels was losing ground and profit. Marketing research showed him that three towels with designs in color and neatly packaged in cardboard containers with transparent tops would sell better and return more profit than lots of a dozen or half dozen less attractively presented.

Surveys and studies show a manufacturer or distributor where to place his marketing effort; where and what kind of dealers to seek, whether to advertise in women's magazines or the television programs women favor, or to appeal to men;

in short, how to direct his entire selling effort. Marketing research enables a company to check on its progress or decline. Using it, a company can find out whether it is maintaining and increasing its share of the market or losing consumer preference and sales to competitors. Sometimes, marketing research can help determine whether a new product should be added to the line or a product that is slipping in popularity be dropped.

Though it is essentially a simple process, marketing research can be, and often is, complex in the techniques it uses and difficult to conduct.

Costly mistakes are possible at every step. If they are not caught and corrected, the results of a survey will be wrong, analysis be incorrect, and marketing based on the faulty research will go wildly and expensively astray. The sample must be accurately representative of the whole group being tested. If it is not, the answers of the few do not indicate the facts about the many. Questions must be phrased so that they are clearly understood, and they cannot be leading questions. Interviewers must all follow exactly the same pattern and keep accurate reports. Whether done by hand or by computer, tabulation must be exact. Analysis of study results must be intelligent and imaginative. If errors are made in any of these basic parts of the entire research operation, the findings are useless and can be damaging. Mistaken or shoddy marketing research is much worse than none at all.

Often, marketing research produces results invaluable to the marketer. They enable him to base his production and distribution plans on facts rather than on guesses. At other times, marketing research merely verifies what the marketer or anyone else with ordinary common sense should have known in the first place. Marketing research is not magic, but it is useful. Like most work, it is only as good as the people who do it.

Though his market was necessarily limited, Robinson Crusoe could have benefited by some elementary marketing research, which really is simply forethought. He spent months of painful effort hollowing a cedar to make a large dugout canoe.

I went to work upon this Boat, the most like a Fool, that ever Man did, who had any of his senses awake. I pleas'd myself with the Design, without determining whether I was ever able to undertake it; not but that the Difficulty of launching my Boat came often into my Head; but I put a stop to my own Enquiries into it, by this foolish Answer which I gave myself. *Let's first make it. I'll warrant I'll find some Way or other to get it along, when 'tis done.*

With infinite labor Crusoe contrived a fine large dugout a hundred yards from shore, with steep sand dunes between it and the water. Try as he might, he could not move his boat. It was not until years later, when Friday and his father came, that Robinson Crusoe could launch his craft.

Sometimes neither the most sophisticated marketing research nor the most expert marketing is effective. Despite marketing's habitual way of looking at them and describing them, consumers are people; and in the end, people seldom make reliable statistics.

People—it is what makes them human—are emotional, irrational, and capable of vagaries few men can foresee. Unexpectedly, they seize on a new fad, then as quickly discard it. They want this, they want that, then they want something entirely different.

The word "want" actually means to lack or to need. Because we usually speak in the strongest possible terms, we use "want" when we really mean wish or desire. A man may want —that is, need—a coat when it is cold, but he is apt to say that he wants a new necktie or to go to a ball game. He does not really need either, any more than a fully clothed woman needs a new dress or a moonstone pendant or a small boy needs a fifth frankfurter after he has just eaten four.

Motorists do not need white sidewall tires on their cars. The car will go just as well on black tires or red ones. A man would like to have white sidewalls because other people have them, because they are more expensive, or because he thinks they would look good on his purple automobile. He keeps thinking about whitewalls, and his desire becomes insistent. He cannot sleep or keep his mind on his work for thinking of them. He will have no peace until he gets them, even if he has to take out another mortgage or sell one of the family. What at first was just a passing wish has become a driving necessity. His desire is now an actual psychological want.

This sounds a little foolish, as perhaps it is, but it is the way we are made. Most of us have the instincts of magpies. We buy and carry off shiny objects which attract. We collect all kinds of things, from campaign buttons and matchbook covers to oil paintings and rare books. We may give other reasons—what we collect has historical, aesthetic, even monetary value—but the real reason is that we wish, then come to want, what we collect.

In one sense, much successful marketing is really the skillful exploitation of human nature, of its needs, appetites, ambitions, vanity, greed, and egoism. Marketing does its best to encourage the competitive impulse which makes a man eager to outdo his friends, neighbors, and enemies; and to make every woman a better wife, mother, motorist, and glamour figure than every other woman.

The changing tastes of people can make a fortune for one marketer and put another out of business. Originally, clothes were worn for protection against the elements. Robinson Crusoe had to devise clothing for this purpose. Long since, clothes have come to be worn mostly for cosmetic purposes. They are decorative and part of sex allure—and they must be in style.

Clothes are also a mark of class distinction. The dishabille of the college student carefully attired in Army-and-Navy store castoffs is a vanity as carefully nurtured as the patched and dirty raggedness of youthful protesters, male and female, against organized society—or the young Wall Street man's conservative uniform of dark suit and quiet tie.

Once older men wore beards because their hands were no

longer steady enough to guide a straight razor. The safety razor was invented, and most men became clean-shaven. Now younger men are affecting beards as a mark of their masculinity and independence or for whatever reason. It may be a passing fancy; it may not be. If it continues, the market for razor blades, the various brands strongly competitive, will fall off sharply.

The market for buggy whips is not what it once was. The telephone, the typewriter, and a more informal way of life have cut severely into the once large market for fine writing papers. A quarter century ago, most homes were heated by soft coal or anthracite. Oil, electricity, and natural gas have largely supplanted coal for home heating. In some states it is illegal to burn coal in the home. These are normal and not unreasonable changes brought about by ordinary circumstances, but some products spring into existence and flourish for a time for no reason at all—the hula hoop, synthetic raccoon-skin caps, knickerbockers for sportswear—then vanish.

For many years, men wore felt hats in fall and winter, straw hats in summer. There were traditional change-over dates. Now, many men, perhaps the majority, wear no hats at all. In the eighteenth century, wigs were for men. In the nineteenth, they were generally for nobody. In the late twentieth, they are for women and even for some fanciful men. It would be difficult to sell a warehouseful of horseshoes now. Once one of the most highly respected of all craftsmen, the blacksmith has practically disappeared. The few remaining blacksmiths ply their trade at race tracks, horse-breeding farms, or riding schools, but that is about all.

There are social and economic changes which affect marketing or which marketing has brought about. It is sometimes difficult to tell which is cause and which is effect.

Once, houses were built to last for forever. Office buildings of stone and steel were expected to last until Doomsday or a few days after. Cars were soundly constructed of heavy metals. The best materials and the best workmanship went into objects of household use. This was a matter of pride with the manufacturer and the worker, and the buyer expected what he bought to last.

Much of this has changed. Houses are hurriedly built. They are meant to last only until a family can afford a better one. Often they do not last that long. Office buildings are expected to become rapidly outmoded. Many structures are erected now with their desertion or demolition ten, twenty, or thirty years hence as part of the original proposal. They will then be supplanted by new buildings incorporating the new materials and conveniences which may be available then. Cars are expected to give satisfactory service for two or three years or a certain number of miles, and sometimes they do.

Quality is not as prized as it was. Buy a cheap dress, shoes, wheelbarrow, or motor. Throw it away and buy a new one. Who wants last year's shoes, outboard, or house trailer? This is the consumer attitude that has made the discount store a success. It panders to the popular and transient.

There is social change manifest in marketing as elsewhere. People have more money to spend, more to spend it on, and more time in which to spend it. The work week is shorter. Vacations are longer and more frequent. There are more paid holidays. Retirement comes earlier.

Modern American society has successfully overcome the fear that all play and no work will make Jack a dull boy and Jill a drip. Dullness and drippiness are the fashion among those who consider themselves the most advanced specimens of our society, and there is a strong market for everything from drugs to jalopies that will provide entertainment of any kind. All the work has been done by previous generations, and all that remains is to enjoy or to joylessly endure.

For the purposes of marketing, eat, drink, and be merry—or miserable—is as good an attitude as any other. It means larger and ever-growing markets for fashion, leisure pursuits, speedy, transportation, food, drink—for everything that contributes or can be thought to contribute to pleasure. Marketing is as ready and willing to serve the hedonist as the puritan. Its concern is that there continue to be markets, that these markets grow, that new markets spring up, and that distribution take care of the whims as well as the wants of consumers.

Undoubtedly, Henry Ford was prompted by humane considerations when in 1914 he shocked industry by introducing his minimum five-dollar-wage for an eight-hour day. A shrewd marketer, he was also well aware that he was expanding the market for his Model-T automobile. His workers, and workers in other industries which would be forced to follow his commanding lead, would have sufficient income to be potential purchasers of Ford cars.

In today's social climate many corporations exercise the same enlightened self-interest. It is a necessity for corporate survival. The need for maintaining free enterprise and protecting business against seizure by the socialized state, the need for an adequate labor supply, the desire to appear as corporate good neighbors, and the need to create, maintain, and enlarge markets—these as well as idealism underlie their contributions to social concerns.

The Xerox Corporation publicizes its development of special on-the-job training for the underprivileged. It aids in trying to help solve community air- and water-pollution problems. It makes annual contributions of large sums of money to charities where it has plants and offices. Yearly, it grants millions of dollars to higher education. The corporation says, "Xerox believes, with many others, that no corporation can exist in isolation from society or from the forces that influence that society. For this reason, we seek to contribute as we can to promote educational enlightenment, economic security, and full freedom of development for everyone."

Federated Department Stores, Inc., urges its executives to participate in community affairs and to work for valid social change. It reiterates its corporate declaration of the acceptance of social responsibility. Federated has established a policy of hiring and training those previously considered unemployable. It costs Federated between $1,000 and $2,500 above normal training expenses to do this, but it does. Ralph Lazarus has said, "There is no longer doubt that business feels it must contribute meaningfully to the social health of the nation," and Federated has acted as well as spoken. It went into partnership with a Negro who had been a basketball All-American to open one of its Ralphs stores in riot-devastated Watts in Los Angeles. The store, a showplace and community center, has a Negro manager, a training center directed by a Negro, and Negro, Mexican-American, and Oriental employees.

J. Paul Austin, president of The Coca-Cola Company, has pointed to the contributions Coca-Cola has made internationally and is continuing to make in helping develop the economies of emerging new countries. It injects capital, production, and marketing skills, and aids in the construction of local industries. It opened a bottling plant in one small African country. Its engineers supervised the building of a glassmaking plant. Coca-Cola paid in advance for a large order, translated its motor-truck manual into the native language, and taught native artisans how to make wooden crates to hold the bottles. The people of the country applied their newly learned skills to other enterprises and developed woodworking, metalworking, and automotive body work and maintenance businesses headed by African managers. The overall results were a sound economy and a stable government.

As long ago as May 15, 1950, when it ran an article on Coca-Cola, *Time* magazine said,

> Its advertising which garnishes the world from the edge of the Arctic Circle to the Cape of Good Hope has created more new appetites and more thirsts in people than an army of dancing girls bearing jugs of wine. It has brought refrigeration to one-ox towns without plumbing and transformed men one generation removed from jungle barter into American salesmen. . . .

Speaking in Detroit in November, 1967, the Coca-Cola president said, "I believe we can imaginatively apply the free enterprise system to combat world poverty. We, the industrial managers, representing multinational businesses, can concentrate our skills and resources to restructure the political and economic cultures of the underdeveloped countries and . . . 'at a profit.' "

At its Copper Cliff smelter in the Sudbury District of Ontario, International Nickel is building the tallest chimney in the world. At 1,250 feet it is about the same height as the Empire State Building in New York. Purpose of the structure, which with related dust-control devices is costing about $13 million, is to dissipate the sulfur dioxide emitted from the smelter—to provide clean air. The company is active in the control of air and water pollution. Increasing recovery of sulfur and sulfur products from smelting and refining benefits both the company and the community.

Laurentian University in Sudbury was founded with the help of a large grant from International Nickel. In Thompson, Manitoba, it built a civic administration building, five schools, a fire station, and a hospital. International Nickel conducts an aid-to-education program in a number of countries. It grants undergraduate scholarships and graduate fellowships in mathematics, metallurgy, and other fields of study in which it has a natural interest, but it also supports study in more general fields, among them educational administration and international relations. The company acknowledges and publicizes recognition of its responsibilities as what it calls "a corporate citizen."

Domestically and internationally, large companies are doing what they can to improve human welfare. They show a genuine concern for people, but they are also intent on bulwarking the free market in the United States and the world.

This interdependence of marketing and human welfare in its largest sense is neither fiction nor idealism but hard fact. Everybody who works for a living lives by marketing. The salesman markets his products, the professional man his skill, the artist his creations. Even the production worker is dependent upon marketing, for if what he makes or helps to make cannot be marketed, it is useless for him or his employer to make it. Production ceases, and both executive and laborer are without earned income.

Everything that is mined, harvested, or made comes out of the earth, the sea, the atmosphere, and man's ingenuity in using it or fashioning what he has found into something of value. Whether it is a necessity or a luxury, a revolutionary device or a child's toy, marketing helps indirectly to produce it. Then, directly, it tells people about it, gets it to them, and persuades them to buy it.

Marketing ensures the consumption that must follow production. When this little pig goes to market, he is performing the consumer's age-old part in the marketing process. Marketing fulfills its responsibilities by seeing to it that the little pig and all the rest of us do not find Mother Hubbard's cupboard bare.

Bibliographical Note

This book is based primarily on government data, the annual reports and other factual information issued by marketing organizations, interviews and correspondence, and the writer's experience. In addition, these publications were drawn upon.

Armstrong, O. K. and Marjorie, "Are Beef Prices Out of Line?" *The Reader's Digest,* April 1970.

Automobile Manufacturers Association, Inc., *Automobiles of America.* Detroit: Wayne State University Press, 1968.

Beckman, Theodore N., and Davidson, William R., *Marketing,* 7th ed. New York: The Ronald Press Co., 1962.

Defoe, Daniel, *The Life and Strange Surprising Adventures of Robinson Crusoe of York, Mariner, as Related by Himself.* London, 1719.

Dewhurst, J. Frederic, and Stewart, Paul W., *Does Distribution Cost Too Much?* New York: Twentieth Century Fund, Inc., 1939.

Duscha, Julius, *Taxpayers' Hayride.* Boston: Little, Brown and Co., 1964.

Fleming, Harold M., *Gasoline Prices and Competition.* New York: Appleton-Century-Crofts, 1966.

Frey, Albert Wesley, ed., *Marketing Handbook,* 2nd ed. New York: The Ronald Press Co., 1965.

Hobart, Donald M., and Wood, J. P., *Selling Forces.* New York: Ronald, 1953.

Levitt, Theodore, *Innovation in Marketing.* New York: McGraw-Hill Book Co., 1962.

Mahoney, Tom, *The Great Merchants.* New York: Harper & Bros., 1955.

Opie, Iona and Peter, eds., *The Oxford Dictionery of Nursery Rhymes.* New York: Oxford University Press, 1951.

Palamountain, Joseph Cornwall, Jr., *The Politics of Distribution*. Cambridge, Massachusetts: Harvard University Press, 1955.

Sorenson, Helen, *The Consumer Movement*. New York: Harper & Bros., 1941.

U.S. Bureau of the Census, *Statistical Abstract of the United States: 1969*. Washington, D. C., 1969.

United States Department of Agriculture, *Compilation of Statutes Relating to Soil Conservation, Marketing Quotas, Allotments*, etc. Agricultural Handbook No. 242. Washington, D. C., 1963.

Wood, James Playsted, *Magazines in the United States*, 3rd ed. New York: Ronald, 1971.

―――― *The Story of Advertising*. New York: Ronald, 1958.

Index

Advertising, 29, 78, 92, 109, 121, 141, 151, 166
Agricultural Trade Development and Assistance Act, 159
Agriculture, United States Department of, 105, 158, 167
Alcott, Amos Bronson, 26
Alice's Adventures Under Ground, 101
Ames Manufacturing Company, 65
Atlantic Monthly, 29
Apperson, Edgar and Elmer, 68
Austin, J. Paul, 182

Baker, Ray Stannard, 168
Bargaining, 75
Barnum & Bailey's Greatest Show on Earth, 67
Bloomingdale's, 123, 130
Bradford, William, 16
Brand names, 28, 87, 102
Brown, Nathan, 36
Burroughs, John, 74

Candler, Asa G., 88
Carlson, Chester, 95
Carroll, Lewis, 101
Centennial Exposition, 37
Clayton Antitrust Act, 156
Coca-Cola Company, The, 88, 161, 182
Collier's, 157
Colt, Samuel, 29
Consumer education, 166
Consumers, 33

Consumers' Research, Inc., 169
Consumers' Union, 170

Defoe, Daniel, 19
Dessauer, Dr. John H., 96
Dexter, Timothy, 31
Discount stores, 124
Disposable personal income, 163
Dollar, value of, 163
Duryea, Charles E., 65
Duryea, J. Frank, 65
Duryea Buggyaut, 66

Edison, Thomas, 74
Emerson, Ralph Waldo, 30

Fair Trade laws, 117, 157
Fairs, 19
Farm price supports, 158
Farms, number and size of, 104
Fashion, 127, 178
Federal Trade Act, 158
Federal Trade Commission, 116, 156, 158
Federated Department Stores, Inc., 122, 161, 181
Field, Marshall, 40
Filene, William, 123
Firestone, Harvey, 74
Food, Drug and Cosmetic Act, 1938; 158
Food and Drug Act, 1906; 157
Ford, Henry, 72, 181
Ford, James T. & Company, 37
Fraser, Charles E., 136
Fraser, Joseph B., 135
Fuoss, Robert M., 127

General Foods Corporation, 111, 160
General Motors Corporation, 161
Gilman, George F., 113
Gimbel Brothers, 41
Good Housekeeping, 167
Great Atlantic & Pacific Tea Company, The, 114, 116, 120
Gresham's Royal Burse, 37

Hartford, George, 114
Hartford, George Huntington, 113
Hartford, John, 114
Herbert, George, 20
Hilton, William, 134
Hilton Head Island, S. C., 134
Holmes, Oliver Wendell, 90
Howe, Elias, Jr., 70

Industrial Revolution, 28
Inflation, 49, 163
Installment buying and selling, 70
International Nickel Company of Canada, Ltd., The, 145, 183

Jordan Marsh and Company, 41

Labeling Acts, 158
Ladies' Home Journal, 157, 166
Laurentian University, 183
Lazarus, Fred, Jr., 123
Lazarus, Ralph, 127, 182
Lumber industry, 57

Macy, Raymond Hussey, 42
Marketing
  automobiles, 64

chain store, 112
channels of distribution, 53
class, 132
communications, 95
definition, 25
department store, 35, 122
direct selling, 75
drugstore, 117
dynamic, 25
exploitation, 178
food, 104
function, 24
history, 13
industrial, 74, 145
mass, 88
real estate, 132
research, 173
restrictions on, 155
Merchant princes, 43
McClure's, 167
McCormick, Silas Hall, 70

Nader, Ralph, 171

O. Henry, 31
Oak Hall, 36
Olds, R. E., 68

Packaging, 50
Peddlers, 26
Pemberton, Dr. John S., 88, 91
Petroleum industry, 55
Philadelphia Public Ledger, 36
Prices, 62
Pricing, 44

Publishing, book, 60

Reader's Digest, The, 171
Rich, Morris, 41
Robinson Crusoe, 13, 21, 176, 178
Robinson-Patman Act, 156

Saks Company, 41
Salesmen, 28, 78, 151
Saturday Evening Post, The, 127
Schlink, F. J., 169
Sea Pines Plantation, 132
Self-service, 117, 124
Selling, direct, 54
Sherman Antitrust Act, 155
Sinclair, Upton, 168
Singer, Isaac, 70
Smith, John, 17
South Carolina Golf Club, 143
Stanley, F. O. and F. E., 68
Steffens, Lincoln, 168
Stewart, A. T., 28, 40
Stourbridge Fair, 19
Sudbury, Ontario, 148, 183
Super Market Institute, 120
Supermarkets, 117, 131
Surpluses, food, 159

Tarbell, Ida, 168
Taxes, 160
Thompson, Manitoba, 148, 183
Time, 182
Transportation, 53
Travelers Insurance Company, The, 140, 142
Twain, Mark, 27

Walton, Izaak, 37
Wanamaker, John, 35, 40
Warne, Colston E., 170
Wholesaling, 55
Wiley, Dr. H. W., 167
Woman's Home Companion, 167
Woodruff, Ernest, 89
Woodruff, Robert W., 89
Woolworth, Frank W., 114

Xerox Corporation, 95, 161, 181